5988 4006

OPPOSING
VIEWPOINTS®
SERIES

Ukraine

Other Books of Related Interest:

Opposing Viewpoints Series

Afghanistan

Syria

US Foreign Policy

World Peace

At Issue Series

Does the World Hate the US?

Foreign Oil Dependence

Immigration Reform

Is China's Economic Growth a Threat to America?

Current Controversies Series

Developing Nations

Immigration

Islamophobia

Pakistan

"Congress shall make
no law . . . abridging
the freedom of speech,
or of the press."

First Amendment to the US Constitution

The basic foundation of our democracy is the First Amendment guarantee of freedom of expression. The Opposing Viewpoints series is dedicated to the concept of this basic freedom and the idea that it is more important to practice it than to enshrine it.

Ukraine

Michael Ruth, Book Editor

GREENHAVEN PRESS
A part of Gale, Cengage Learning

GALE
CENGAGE Learning·

Farmington Hills, Mich • San Francisco • New York • Waterville, Maine
Meriden, Conn • Mason, Ohio • Chicago

GALE
CENGAGE Learning

Judy Galens, *Manager, Frontlist Acquisitions*

© 2016 Greenhaven Press, a part of Gale, Cengage Learning.

Gale and Greenhaven Press are registered trademarks used herein under license.

For more information, contact:
Greenhaven Press
27500 Drake Rd.
Farmington Hills, MI 48331-3535
Or you can visit our Internet site at gale.cengage.com

For product information and technology assistance, contact us at

Gale Customer Support, 1-800-877-4253
For permission to use material from this text or product, submit all requests online at
www.cengage.com/permissions

Further permissions questions can be emailed to permissionrequest@cengage.com

Articles in Greenhaven Press anthologies are often edited for length to meet page requirements. In addition, original titles of these works are changed to clearly present the main thesis and to explicitly indicate the author's opinion. Every effort is made to ensure that Greenhaven Press accurately reflects the original intent of the authors. Every effort has been made to trace the owners of copyrighted material.

Cover Image copyright © Labrador Photo Video/Shutterstock.com.

LIBRARY OF CONGRESS CATALOGING-IN-PUBLICATION DATA

Names: Ruth, Michael (Book editor)
Title: Ukraine (Greenhaven Press) / Michael Ruth, book editor.
Description: Farmington Hills, Mich. : Greenhaven Press, a part of Gale, Cengage Learning, 2016. | Series: Opposing viewpoints | Includes bibliographical references and index.
Identifiers: LCCN 2015024215 | ISBN 9780737775648 (hardback) | ISBN 9780737775655 (paperback)
Subjects: LCSH: Ukraine Conflict, 2014- | Military assistance, American--Ukraine. | National security--Ukraine. | Self-determination, Ukraine--Foreign relations--1991- | Russia (Federation)--Foreign relations--21st century. | United States--Foreign relations--2009- | BISAC: JUVENILE NONFICTION / Social Science / Politics & Government.
Classification: LCC DK508.852 .U39 2016 | DDC 947.7086--dc23
LC record available at http://lccn.loc.gov/2015024215

Printed in the United States of America
1 2 3 4 5   19 18 17 16 15

Contents

Chapter 2: Should the West Intervene in Ukraine?

Chapter 3: What Should Be Russia's Place in Ukraine?

Chapter 4: How Should Ukraine Plan Its Future?

Why Consider Opposing Viewpoints?

"The only way in which a human being can make some approach to knowing the whole of a subject is by hearing what can be said about it by persons of every variety of opinion and studying all modes in which it can be looked at by every character of mind. No wise man ever acquired his wisdom in any mode but this."

John Stuart Mill

In our media-intensive culture it is not difficult to find differing opinions. Thousands of newspapers and magazines and dozens of radio and television talk shows resound with differing points of view. The difficulty lies in deciding which opinion to agree with and which "experts" seem the most credible. The more inundated we become with differing opinions and claims, the more essential it is to hone critical reading and thinking skills to evaluate these ideas. Opposing Viewpoints books address this problem directly by presenting stimulating debates that can be used to enhance and teach these skills. The varied opinions contained in each book examine many different aspects of a single issue. While examining these conveniently edited opposing views, readers can develop critical thinking skills such as the ability to compare and contrast authors' credibility, facts, argumentation styles, use of persuasive techniques, and other stylistic tools. In short, the Opposing Viewpoints Series is an ideal way to attain the higher-level thinking and reading skills so essential in a culture of diverse and contradictory opinions.

In addition to providing a tool for critical thinking, Opposing Viewpoints books challenge readers to question their own strongly held opinions and assumptions. Most people form their opinions on the basis of upbringing, peer pressure, and personal, cultural, or professional bias. By reading carefully balanced opposing views, readers must directly confront new ideas as well as the opinions of those with whom they disagree. This is not to argue simplistically that everyone who reads opposing views will—or should—change his or her opinion. Instead, the series enhances readers' understanding of their own views by encouraging confrontation with opposing ideas. Careful examination of others' views can lead to the readers' understanding of the logical inconsistencies in their own opinions, perspective on why they hold an opinion, and the consideration of the possibility that their opinion requires further evaluation.

Evaluating Other Opinions

To ensure that this type of examination occurs, Opposing Viewpoints books present all types of opinions. Prominent spokespeople on different sides of each issue as well as well-known professionals from many disciplines challenge the reader. An additional goal of the series is to provide a forum for other, less known, or even unpopular viewpoints. The opinion of an ordinary person who has had to make the decision to cut off life support from a terminally ill relative, for example, may be just as valuable and provide just as much insight as a medical ethicist's professional opinion. The editors have two additional purposes in including these less known views. One, the editors encourage readers to respect others' opinions—even when not enhanced by professional credibility. It is only by reading or listening to and objectively evaluating others' ideas that one can determine whether they are worthy of consideration. Two, the inclusion of such viewpoints encourages the important critical thinking skill of objectively evaluating an author's credentials and bias. This evaluation will illuminate an author's reasons for taking a particular stance on an issue and will aid in readers' evaluation of the author's ideas.

It is our hope that these books will give readers a deeper understanding of the issues debated and an appreciation of the complexity of even seemingly simple issues when good and honest people disagree. This awareness is particularly important in a democratic society such as ours in which people enter into public debate to determine the common good. Those with whom one disagrees should not be regarded as enemies but rather as people whose views deserve careful examination and may shed light on one's own.

Thomas Jefferson once said that "difference of opinion leads to inquiry, and inquiry to truth." Jefferson, a broadly educated man, argued that "if a nation expects to be ignorant and free . . . it expects what never was and never will be." As individuals and as a nation, it is imperative that we consider the opinions of others and examine them with skill and discernment. The Opposing Viewpoints series is intended to help readers achieve this goal.

David L. Bender and Bruno Leone,
Founders

Introduction

"Pro-Russian separatists are fighting government forces in eastern Ukraine, demanding autonomy from Kiev and in rebellion against the overthrow of President Viktor Yanukovych in February [2014]. More than one million people have been displaced by the conflict, which has raised underlying tensions between ethnic Ukrainians, Russians and other minorities in the former Soviet republic."

—Lizzie Dearden,
*"Ukraine Crisis: A Timeline
of the Conflict from the
Euromaidan Protests to MH17
and Civil War in the East,"*
Independent, *September 2, 2014*

As the Soviet Union was breaking up in 1989, a wave of democratic revolutions spread throughout Eastern Europe, and Soviet satellite states such as Poland, Hungary, and Czechoslovakia wholly rejected communism in favor of the kinds of socially liberal democracies of the Western world. Even before the Soviet Union officially dissolved in 1991, many of these countries had already thrown off the fifty-year authoritarian rule of their former dominator and had begun implementing democratic reforms. The Cold War—which since the mid-1940s had pitted the United States and Western Europe against the Soviet Union for military, political, and economic dominance of world affairs—had now ended.

Amid the ongoing Eastern European protests in mid-1989, the American political scientist Francis Fukuyama published an essay titled "The End of History?" in the international affairs magazine *National Interest*. In it, he argued that the grand ideological struggle between the despotic communism of the Eastern world and the liberal democracies of the West had ended in democratic victory. The strongest, most successful nations in the world, Fukuyama argued, were democracies that respected human rights and supported free economies, while Soviet-style dictatorships simply could never last. In this regard, Fukuyama believed, political history had finally reached its end, with liberal democracy proven to be the greatest form of human society ever established.

In the years following the publication of Fukuyama's 1992 book *The End of History and the Last Man*, the idea of the end of history was questioned numerous times by those who witnessed certain world events that blatantly violated Fukuyama's declaration. If political history had ended in Western liberalism's triumph, critics asked, how could incidents such as the September 11, 2001, terrorist attacks on the United States be explained? What accounted for the post-9/11 spread of global Islamic extremism? According to these objectors, the world still produced plenty of examples of the continuing ideological battle between democracy and oppressive totalitarianism.

In 2014 some critics referred to the Russian invasion and annexation of the Ukrainian peninsula of Crimea as yet another case of a nondemocratic philosophy challenging the supremacy of Western-style democracy. The event had begun unfolding in November of 2013, when Ukrainians staged mass protests against the corrupt administration of President Viktor Yanukovych, whom protesters forced out of office in February of 2014. Ostensibly to protect the interests of the ethnic Russian majority in Crimea from the newly elected pro-Western Ukrainian government, Russian president Vladimir Putin ordered the Russian military to occupy the peninsula and protect the autonomous parliament while it voted to secede from

Ukraine and join Russia. Following Russia's annexation of Crimea, an armed conflict broke out in southeastern Ukraine between the Ukrainian military and Russian-supplied separatists attempting to form their own independent republics.

In the midst of what was perceived as Russia's militaristic aggression against Ukraine, Fukuyama was again challenged on whether his proclamation that history had ended still applied to the twenty-first-century world. His adamant response was that it did, in the context of the philosophical definition of history. Fukuyama explained this in a 2014 interview with the German broadcast news service Deutsche Welle:

> History, in the philosophical sense, is really the development, or the evolution—or the modernization—of institutions, and the question is: In the world's most developed societies, what type [of institutions] are they? I think it's pretty clear that any society that wants to be modern still needs to have a combination of democratic political institutions in a market economy. And I don't think that China, or Russia, or any of the competitors out there really undermine that point.

Fukuyama's statement was supported by assertions from his own book, in which he stated that the end of history did not entail that no major international events would ever occur again, but only that no other political philosophy could ever seriously compete with liberal democracy. An aggressive Russia seeking and claiming the territory of the sovereign nation of Ukraine, Fukuyama argued to Deutsche Welle in 2014, demonstrated that geopolitics, or international relations based on geographic location, still played a role in world affairs. He concluded, however, that Russia was economically weak and not a true democracy and, therefore, could not be regarded as an ideological threat to Western liberalism.

As Ukraine's war with Russian-supported rebels continued into 2015, some commentators persisted in referring to the conflict as a new Cold War, with Ukraine as a battleground for the ongoing clash between freedom and geopolitical aggression. Others, such as Fukuyama, dismissed such claims, saying that Ukraine's standoff with Russia was strictly regional and did not represent another global contest for ideological dominance.

Opposing Viewpoints: Ukraine presents the views of numerous authors on questions relating to the Ukraine crisis. The important issues of Ukraine's current political status in the world are addressed in chapters titled "How Should the United States Manage the Ukraine Conflict?," "Should the West Intervene in Ukraine?," "What Should Be Russia's Place in Ukraine?," and "How Should Ukraine Plan Its Future?"

OPPOSING
VIEWPOINTS®
SERIES

CHAPTER 1

How Should the United States Manage the Ukraine Conflict?

Chapter Preface

U kraine established formal diplomatic relations with the United States in 1991, the year it became an independent republic following decades of Communist rule by the Soviet Union. This new American friendship was important during Ukraine's difficult early years as a fledgling democracy, as it attempted to emerge from the political and economic ruin of its Communist past and become a viable player on the international stage.

American-Ukrainian diplomacy throughout the 1990s focused on a number of key political components on which the United States vowed to collaborate with Ukraine. These included national defense and security, the country's energy sector, the establishment of democratic institutions, and international trade for strengthening the Ukrainian economy. With the United States' help, and its own internal efforts to democratize, Ukraine had begun transforming into a democratic state within only a few years, holding presidential elections in 1994 and ratifying a democratic constitution in 1996.

Amiable relations between Ukraine and the United States continued into the 2010s, especially concerning economic cooperation. Today, the United States regularly exports coal, automobiles, heavy machinery, aircraft, and seafood to Ukraine, while Ukraine sells the United States oil, inorganic chemicals, agricultural products, and both raw and unfinished iron and steel products—the country's main industry. Additionally, 2008's United States–Ukraine Charter on Strategic Partnership reiterated the two countries' commitments to cooperation on democracy, security, defense, and energy.

In 2013, when Ukrainians began protesting their president, Viktor Yanukovych, for abandoning a long-discussed economic partnership with the European Union in favor of a different deal with Russia, the United States spoke out in favor of

Ukrainian citizens' calling for a Western-style democracy. In February of 2014, increasing protester violence in the Ukrainian capital of Kiev forced Yanukovych to flee the country, allowing the parliament to elect a new, pro-Western government to lead Ukraine through its political upheaval.

In response to Ukraine's apparent turn toward the West, Russian president Vladimir Putin, who viewed Ukraine's friendship with the West as a national security threat to his own country, ordered the Russian military to invade the autonomous Ukrainian peninsula of Crimea and oversee a parliamentary election there on the question of secession. As the majority of the Crimean people were ethnic Russians, the secession vote passed, and Russia effectively stole Crimea from Ukraine in March of 2014. Armed conflict then erupted in Ukraine's southern and eastern regions between the national military and Russian-supported rebels fighting for independence from Ukraine. The conflict had left more than six thousand people dead by March of 2015.

Throughout this sequence of events, which collectively became known as the Ukraine crisis, the United States harshly condemned Russia's actions while emphatically supporting Ukraine's right to determine its own political future. In March of 2014, US secretary of state John Kerry traveled to Kiev to present the new Ukrainian government with a $1 billion loan from the United States to help the country through its financial hardship. Later that month, President Barack Obama hosted Ukrainian prime minister Arseniy Yatsenyuk at the White House to show American solidarity with the Ukrainian people. The fighting in Ukraine continued into 2015.

The following chapter presents multiple views on how the United States should assist Ukraine with its ongoing political crisis. Topics discussed include whether the United States should militarily defend Ukraine from Russia, provide weapons to the Ukrainian army, continue imposing economic sanctions on Russia, and support the Minsk agreement for peace in the Ukrainian conflict.

> *"The simple truth is that the West can defend Ukraine from further Russian invasion and do so without a prolonged conflict."*

The United States Should Intervene Militarily in the Ukraine Conflict

Jorge Benitez

In the following viewpoint, Jorge Benitez argues that the United States can and should help Ukraine defend itself from Russian aggression. Ukraine is a key Western ally, Benitez believes, one that, in the future, could stand up to further Russian military incursions into Western Europe. Stopping Russia in Ukraine, Benitez contends, would potentially save a great deal of effort stopping it elsewhere in the world later. Benitez is director of the NATOSource blog and a senior fellow at the Atlantic Council.

As you read, consider the following questions:

1. What five Western military elements does Benitez suggest combining to intervene against Russia in Ukraine?

2. What area of Russia does Benitez say the West should not initially attack?

3. What two other European countries does Benitez suggest Vladimir Putin might attempt to stop from joining NATO?

It is becoming harder and harder to ignore Russia's growing military intervention in Ukraine. The diplomatic and economic efforts of President Barack Obama and European leaders have failed to stop Russian president Vladimir Putin's repeated escalation of this crisis. It is irresponsible to not examine how the West can use a limited amount of force to prevent Russia from conquering more of Ukraine. No matter how reluctant transatlantic leaders are to consider military options, the simple truth is that the West can defend Ukraine from further Russian invasion and do so without a prolonged conflict.

The key element of this military option is the important distinction that it only involves using force against Russian units attacking Ukraine. This is a defensive military option to protect Ukraine and stop Russian aggression in another country. It is not an offensive military option; only Russian forces beyond Russia's borders would be targeted. It would not be a military threat to Russia or the Russian people.

A Western Alliance

The most feasible military option to help defend Ukraine would be a combination of Western air power, special forces, intelligence, remotely powered aircraft (aka drones) and cyberpower. This limited military option requires few boots on the ground and is comparable to the options used to initially defeat larger enemy forces in Afghanistan and Libya. This will not be a NATO [North Atlantic Treaty Organization] mission, because it is improbable that all 28 members of the alliance would authorize this option. Nevertheless, a transatlantic coalition led by the U.S., Britain, France, Poland and Romania could host and deploy a more than adequate force multiplier to help the Ukrainian military defeat and repel Russian troops from their territory.

This option would require a major investment of allied air power. Russian forces in Ukraine will offer significantly more effective opposition than previous coalitions faced in Serbia, Afghanistan, Iraq and Libya. But the West does have the military capability to overcome this sophisticated adversary. In fact, Europe could defeat Russian forces without U.S. assistance if its leaders had the political will to act together and share the costs. If pooled together, Europe's national air forces have more combat planes than Russia has available west of the Urals [a mountain range in western Russia]. Even in the case of a full-scale Russian invasion of Ukraine, Putin will need to keep major portions of the Russian military protecting the border in the Far East, Central Asia, the Caucasus and the Baltic region. The combination of willing European allies with U.S. military capabilities would prove more than a match for the limited forces Putin could pour into Ukraine.

It is necessary to acknowledge one important caveat to this option's exclusion of Russian territory from Western attacks and that is Kaliningrad, the Russian port on the Baltic. The West should initially respect Russian control over Kaliningrad. But if Russian forces from Kaliningrad or elsewhere in Russian territory use force against coalition territory or forces (including Ukraine), then Kaliningrad would lose its protection and become a legitimate target for coalition attacks.

Too High a Risk?

There are some that will feel that this military option is too provocative. They will strongly oppose any direct military combat between Western forces and the Russian military. Critics will also fear that this military option will lead to even more dangerous escalation of the crisis. The political decision to use force deserves to be taken cautiously, but such caution should not incapacitate national leaders from objectively examining the potential of a military option to do what current diplomatic and economic options have failed to do: stop Putin and save Ukraine.

We should also remember that this would not be the first time Western and Russian forces fought against each other. Moscow sent Russian air power to oppose U.N. [United Nations] and U.S. forces in Korea and China sent hundreds of thousands of its troops to turn the tide in that conflict. By limiting combat to the Korean peninsula, the great powers clashed but collectively prevented the conflict from escalating into total war.

The use of force against Russian units attacking Ukraine does involve risk and loss of life. But so does our current policy of diplomatic condemnation and limited economic sanctions. Week after week, transatlantic leaders repeat their warnings to Putin, but he continues to escalate the crisis and the death toll in Ukraine rises.

It is highly unlikely that this military option will ever receive serious consideration from Obama and most European leaders. They prefer to communicate to Moscow that all military options are off the table for the West, even as Putin sends more Russian military hardware and personnel into Ukraine. Nevertheless, the case needs to be made for a proportional response to Putin's actions.

Putin's Ambition

One of the main reasons why the West should be willing to undertake the risks and costs of this military option is that Putin will not stop after he takes what he wants from Ukraine. As he has done against Estonia, Georgia and Crimea, Putin will continue to coerce and attack his weak neighbors as long as he can do so without a strong response from the West. Will he next try to "protect" ethnic Russians in energy-rich Kazakhstan or expand Russian control beyond Transnistria to take over all of Moldova?

Or will Putin try to block the alliance choices of other neighbors? For example, Sweden and Finland are both closer to NATO membership than Ukraine. Russia's opposition to them joining NATO is almost as strong as it is to Kiev's relationship with NATO. Could Putin someday overreact to Stockholm and Helsinki's partnership with NATO and initiate another "frozen conflict" to keep Sweden and Finland out of the alliance?

Putin has communicated clearly and repeatedly that he is willing to use force to resolve disputes and that he will intervene to "protect" Russians living in neighboring countries. Western leaders wanted to believe that the invasion of Georgia would not be repeated and that Putin would be content with Crimea. But Putin continues to defy their hopes for peace with increasing use of Russian military power. NATO leaders must ask themselves, if Putin wins militarily against Ukraine, will he stop there or will Russia be more likely to use force later against another of its neighbors?

A Hard Choice

The cyber campaigns and increased covert intelligence efforts that preceded Russia's seizure of the Crimea are already being conducted elsewhere in Europe, including within NATO members. Few observers delude themselves that Putin's emphasis on surprise 24-hour military mobilizations and exercises are being done for defensive purposes, especially after seeing the unexpected speed with which the Russian military acted against Ukraine.

If Putin's aggression is not stopped in Ukraine, it will cost the West much more in lives and resources to stop him elsewhere. No other vulnerable state along Russia's borders has the geostrategic depth and value of Ukraine. Ukraine also has the largest pro-West population to defend against Russian invasion.

The military option to save Ukraine from further Russian occupation should not be dismissed perfunctorily by Obama and European leaders. The military defense of Ukraine deserves at least a serious debate and top-level consideration.

> "It's time for America to stop policing the world, and start its exodus from Europe."

The United States Should Stay Out of the Ukraine Conflict

Chris Freind

In the following viewpoint, Chris Freind argues that the United States should avoid the Ukraine-Russia conflict at all costs, for it is not America's concern. It would be arrogant and inappropriate, Freind writes, for a country as young as the United States to attempt to understand centuries-old ethnic ties between European nations such as Ukraine and Russia. Doing so, he contends, would lead to a long and unnecessary war in Eastern Europe that no nation wants. Freind is an independent columnist and commentator.

As you read, consider the following questions:

1. What two other conflicted nations does Freind cite as examples of why the United States cannot understand the cultural ties between Ukraine and Russia?

2. What perception of America does Freind say results from a misguided interventionist foreign policy?

3. What three American actions does Freind say would antagonize Russian president Vladimir Putin into escalating the Ukrainian crisis?

S tay away. Far, far away.

Unless America wants to see the powder keg of Europe ignited once again—and it's not a stretch to say that actively opposing Russia in its conflict with Ukraine could potentially start World War III—it will steer clear of that region. Avoiding another global war (this time with nuclear weapons) should be reason enough, but here's another one: It's not our fight.

Right now, it is a limited brawl between those two nations, and, despite the spin that Russia is the bad guy, it is not at all clear who is "right." Either way, those powerful nations dominate that region; we don't. To march in as a self-righteous superpower thinking we can "fix" the problem is arrogant, naïve—and dangerous.

Let's analyze the situation.

Civilian Airplane Shot Down

1.) Malaysia Airlines: They have now lost two 777s in the past couple of months. It's enough to bankrupt any airline. In a span of four months, Malaysia Airlines planes have been involved in two of the worst airline tragedies in decades.

In the first incident, the jury remains out on just what happened to the missing Flight 370. While some conspiracy theories are absurd, others cannot be so easily dismissed. One thing is certain: The problems that have dogged the Malaysian government and Malaysia Airlines officials were on full display after Flight 370's disappearance. A few months later, most experts believe Flight 17 was blown out of the sky by a surface-to-air missile. The tragedy over the Ukraine took place even after airlines had been repeatedly warned since April [2014] to avoid flying over that conflicted region. The Malaysian jet failed to heed that warning.

2.) Apparently the concept of "innocent until proven guilty" has been lost on many American leaders clamoring for more action against the pro-Russian rebels and Russia itself. Last time we checked, it remains unclear who fired the missile, especially since the Ukraine military operates the exact same SA-11 system.

And it's not unprecedented for missiles to be fired at the wrong targets. Iraq killed 37 sailors on the USS *Stark* in 1987 when one of its airplane missiles mistakenly hit the Navy frigate. Similarly, the American cruiser [USS] *Vincennes* mistakenly shot down an Iranian airliner, killing nearly 300 people in 1988. We can't have it both ways, stating that the Malaysian jet was unmistakably a passenger jet, yet excusing how one of the world's most sophisticated radar systems (Aegis [Combat System]) thought a jumbo jet was a small, attacking fighter. Our credibility on the world stage is at stake, so let's think before we speak.

Not America's Problem

3.) The question of which country the predominantly Russian-speaking people of Crimea want to be aligned with is not new; these ethnic and nationality issues don't just transcend borders, but time, with allegiances going back hundreds, even thousands, of years. We are a nation barely over 200 years old, with absolutely no concept of how far back, and how strong, these European ties are. To think we can provide the solution is naïveté at its worst.

We used the same approach for engaging Iraq and Afghanistan. How's that working out for us?

4.) Here a news flash: The Cold War [referring to political and military tension between the United States and the Soviet

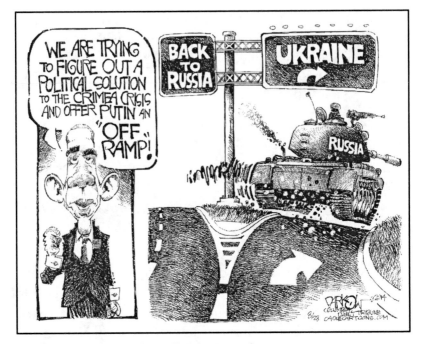

Union after World War II until 1991] is over. For those war-mongers who missed it, perhaps we should declare victory again and move on, and out, of Europe. It's been pointed out here before it's time for America to stop policing the world, and start its exodus from Europe. Only four NATO [North Atlantic Treaty Organization] countries meet their paltry requirement for defense spending, yet the U.S. always exceeds its obligation to pick up the slack. If the Russian-Ukrainian conflict is anybody's business, it's Europe's. It falls entirely within their sphere of influence, so let them deal with it.

That's not to advocate isolationism, as it is in America's interest to have a global presence. But an aggressive and all-too-often misguided interventionist foreign policy (one advocated by both parties) leaves the perception of the U.S. as imperialistic aggressors, which creates exponentially more problems down the road. Time to stop expending blood and treasure in foreign lands while our protectees default on their end of the bargain, leaving us holding an empty bag.

5.) We haven't done too well choosing sides in other regional conflicts. We backed the Libyan rebels (the largest foreign force in Iraq to fight the U.S., by the way) who overthrew [Libyan dictator] Moammar Gadhafi, after which 10,000 surface-to-air missiles disappeared and the Benghazi tragedy [referring to the 2012 attacks by Islamic militants on the American diplomatic compound in Benghazi, Libya, killing four Americans and seven Libyans] occurred. Bet the ranch neither would have happened had Gadhafi remained in power.

We are backing the Syrian rebels, who are unquestionably more radical and anti-American than the government of Bashar [al-]Assad; the Iraqi government we helped install is worthless; and Afghani president Hamid Karzai is astonishingly ungrateful. Instead of meddling in foreign affairs so much, maybe it's time to focus on the people who should matter most: Americans. In America.

No Political Solution

6.) You know we've reached a low point when politicians bash the other side just to score cheap political points for some perceived gain, especially when doing so risks an expanded armed conflict in Europe, potentially putting American lives on the line.

For those hammering President Obama (with some even blaming him for the Malaysian shoot down), one question: What exactly do you want him to do? Send "advisers" to the Ukraine, which always leads to more troops? Send more navy ships to the region? Arm the Ukraine to the hilt? All will antagonize Russian leader Vladimir Putin and cause him to escalate the crisis. We cannot win a war there. Period. Since the outcome doesn't affect us, let's wait this one out on the sidelines.

Western Intervention in Ukraine

Samantha Power, the U.S. ambassador to the United Nations, recently cautioned Americans against intervention fatigue: "I think there is too much of 'Oh, look, this is what intervention has wrought' . . . one has to be careful about overdrawing lessons." Say what? Given the calamities wrought in Iraq, Libya and now Ukraine, one would think that a fundamental rethinking and learning of lessons is long overdue. The United States needs a sober look at the actual costs of supposed good intentions divorced from realism. . . .

One year after the United States and Europe celebrated the February [2014] coup that ousted the corrupt but constitutionally elected president of Ukraine, Viktor Yanukovych, liberal and neoconservative interventionists have much to answer for. Crimea has been annexed by Russia. More than 4,000 people have lost their lives in the civil war in Ukraine, with more than 9,000 wounded and nearly a million displaced. . . .

No one will fight for eastern Ukraine except the Ukrainians and presumably the Russians. . . . The hawks should stand down. The human costs are already mounting. It is utterly irresponsible to destroy a country in the name of supporting it, as is happening in Ukraine. Samantha Power has it wrong: Americans aren't tired of humanitarian intervention; they are tired of its consequences. It is time for taking a sober look at the misconceptions that got us here.

Katrina vanden Heuvel,
"Rethinking the Cost of Western Intervention in Ukraine,"
Washington Post, *Nov. 25, 2014.*

As far as sanctions, good luck standing alone, Western Europe chose not to become energy independent, or at least dependent on friendly nations like Canada and the U.S. (which could be energy independent but is not). So it must rely on the Middle East, and even more so, Russia, for its lifeblood: natural gas. Watch for them to cheat on, or rescind, any sanctions.

Putin's economy is sliding, but his people are rallying behind him and he is holding the better cards. Let Europe figure this one out.

Russia is not the superpower it once was, but it is still a powerful player that must be respected (after all, it's the only ticket to our space station, but that's another story). Warmongers' cries of "appeasement" notwithstanding, playing "chicken-Kiev" with Russia is not sound foreign policy. It's a recipe for disaster.

"Is the perceived need to confront Putin in Ukraine a more important American national interest than ending the Iranian nuclear crisis?"

If U.S. Arms Ukraine, Russia Could Arm Iran

Josh Cohen

In the following viewpoint, Josh Cohen argues that the United States should not arm Ukraine against Russia, for Russia could retaliate by arming Iran, a dangerous prospect for America. An increase in Ukrainian arms, Cohen writes, would force Russian president Vladimir Putin to escalate the conflict in Ukraine, leading to further loss of life. When an armed Iran is added to this situation, Cohen believes, the proposition of the United States arming Ukraine appears wholly unwise. Cohen is a former US State Department project officer and a current contributor to foreign policy media outlets.

As you read, consider the following questions:

1. In what way does Cohen compare Russia and Ukraine to China and Taiwan?

2. What does Cohen say would happen if Iran acquired the Russian S-400 air defense system?

3. How else besides the arming of Iran does Cohen say Putin could retaliate for the United States arming Ukraine?

The war drums are once again beating in Washington. An attention-grabbing report released by three of America's leading think tanks recommends that the United States save Ukraine by arming it. The U.S. government, the report argues, should alter its policy and begin providing lethal assistance to Ukraine's military—$3 billion over the next three years. That is serious money.

The rationale used by Washington's legion of escalation focuses on the notion of "raising the costs for Putin." If Kiev had advanced weaponry, so the argument goes, it would be able to inflict higher casualties on the Russian troops Putin has apparently sent into the Donbass to support the separatists there. Boiled down to its essence then, the idea is that an increase in Russian soldiers coming home from Ukraine in body bags will force Putin to back down to prevent a domestic backlash.

While it is easy to see the seductive simplicity of this reasoning, let's not forget that if the U.S. raises the ante, Putin will almost certainly do the same in Ukraine and elsewhere. First and foremost, the pro-escalation argument greatly underestimates the lengths Putin would be willing to go to in Ukraine.

Since the first stirrings on Kiev's Maidan, the West has consistently overlooked the tremendous importance of Ukraine to Russia. Russia views Ukraine similarly to how China looks at Taiwan: as an existential issue in which certain red lines must not be crossed.

For Putin, the overthrow of former Ukrainian president Viktor Yanukovych risked opening the door for Ukraine to join NATO and the Western alliance system—something which Moscow could not and will never accept. All of Putin's moves since then have been intended to prevent this.

Once we understand that Ukraine's status is an existential issue for Moscow, it is clear that Putin will never allow the separatists to be defeated—and indeed Russia possesses the military might to ensure that this never happens. In this regard, Putin possesses what analysts referred to during the Cold War as "escalation dominance," described by American nuclear strategist Herman Kahn as "a capacity, other things being equal, to enable the side possessing it to enjoy marked advantages in a given region of the escalation ladder."

Put simply, in Ukraine Putin enjoys escalation dominance at every level of the potential military escalation chain, and no amount of wishful thinking will change this fact.

Consider what happened in late August when it appeared as though the Ukrainian military might rout the separatists. In response to Kiev's escalation, Putin escalated as well, sending in enough Russian troops and heavy weaponry to inflict a bloody defeat on the Ukrainian forces at Ilovaisk.

Likewise, Putin would almost certainly respond to an increase in Kiev's military capabilities now by doubling down on Russia's military support for the separatists. In a worst-case scenario Russia could perhaps even invade Ukraine outright.

The end result would be even greater death and destruction in the Donbass, with the possibility of a settlement even further away—the exact opposite outcome the West would have intended.

Another fact overlooked by those in favor of arming Kiev is that Putin could choose to escalate asymmetrically, outside of Ukraine. Iran would be the worst case. In late January, Russian defense minister Sergei Shoigu visited Iran and signed a military cooperation pact with Tehran.

One item from this trip was particularly alarming. Retired Russian general Leonid Ivashov summarized the Tehran meet-

The United States Should Not Arm Ukraine

President Barack Obama has resisted demands to escalate our response to Russia's aggression against Ukraine, but his resistance may soon collapse. . . .

This week [in February 2015], a report from three establishment-oriented think tanks—the Atlantic Council, the Brookings Institution and the Chicago Council on Global Affairs—said the United States should provide "lethal defensive arms" and other supplies to the Kiev government. Ashton Carter, nominated to be secretary of defense, said in his confirmation hearing Wednesday, "I'm very much inclined in that direction."

But Obama abstained from shipping weapons to Ukraine because there was no reason to think they would do much good—and there still isn't. Lethal military assistance combines several unappealing features. It would cost a lot of money that would probably be wasted, since the arms would not be sufficient to stop Vladimir Putin from achieving any military goal he sets. It could induce him to intensify his aggression before our help can arrive.

It could expand the destruction of the fighting without changing the outcome. And it's likely to eventually present the U.S. with a choice between accepting defeat and having to use our own forces to save Ukraine. . . .

The problem is that the U.S. has neither the means nor the motivation to stop Putin. Ukraine is always going to be a lot closer to Moscow than to Washington, and its fate is always going to matter a lot more to the Russians than to us.

Steve Chapman, "Why We Shouldn't Arm Ukraine,"
Reason.com, February 5, 2015.

ings, noting that "a step was taken in the direction of cooperation on the economy and arms technology, at least for such defensive systems as the S-300 and S-400. Probably we will deliver them."

With a radius of 400 kilometers and an ability to shoot down cruise missiles as well as aircraft, the Center for Strategic and International Studies describes the S-400 as "Russia's most advanced air defense system . . . designed specifically to contest U.S. air superiority." Though Ivashov is a controversial figure, this is dangerous stuff, and in Iranian hands it could potentially change the balance of power in the Middle East.

Russia has been involved in on-again, off-again negotiations to sell these missiles to Iran, first the S-300 and now the S-400. To date, Moscow has held off on actually completing the sale, at least partially so as not to undermine the prospects for the P5+1 to reach a comprehensive nuclear deal with Tehran.

While the focus of the P5+1 has been to achieve a peaceful resolution to the Iranian nuclear crisis, the threat of a U.S. or Israeli military strike on Tehran's nuclear facilities has hung in the background as a possibility if talks fail.

However the Israelis are already distrustful of America's commitment to ending Iran's nuclear program, and if it appeared that Tehran was about to deploy S-400 missiles, the Israelis might well choose to strike Iran unilaterally, plunging the Middle East into a horrific conflict.

For a Kremlin concerned with global stability, a nuclear Iran or a Middle East war is certainly not something Moscow would desire. In the context of Ukraine, however, don't underestimate Putin's willingness to play the Iran card.

Speaking last year after one P5+1 negotiating session in Switzerland, Deputy Foreign Minister Sergei Ryabkov said: "We wouldn't like to use these talks as an element of the game of raising the stakes in Ukraine . . . but if they force us into that, we will take retaliatory measures here as well."

In this context, before embarking on a policy specifically designed to kill Russian troops with American weapons, Washington well might ask itself the following question: Is the perceived need to confront Putin in Ukraine a more important American national interest than ending the Iranian nuclear crisis?

Moreover, Iran is just one locale where Putin could retaliate for the shipment of American weaponry to Kiev. Moscow could escalate nuclear tensions within Europe too. Russia could start by withdrawing from the Intermediate-Range Nuclear Forces Treaty, a 1987 pact that eliminated all of the United States' and former Soviet Union's nuclear and conventional ground-launched ballistic and cruise missiles with ranges of 500 to 5,500 kilometers.

Russia has already moved 10 nuclear-capable Iskander missiles with a range of 400 kilometers into Kaliningrad, as well as terminated an agreement with Lithuania to provide information to Vilnius about Russian weaponry in Kaliningrad.

The next step—if Russia were to withdraw from the INF pact—would be to explicitly announce that nuclear missiles capable of striking anywhere in Europe were now deployed to Kaliningrad. If Russia and the West are not already involved in a full-scale cold war, this would certainly do the trick.

U.S. president Barack Obama once described a key criterion guiding his foreign policy as "don't do stupid stuff." Sending billions of dollars in lethal arms to Kiev would violate this maxim in spades.

> "By sending arms to Ukraine, Washington will be sending Moscow a clear message that it cannot threaten its neighbors with impunity."

The United States Should Arm Ukraine

Luke Coffey and Nile Gardiner

In the following viewpoint, Luke Coffey and Nile Gardiner argue that the United States should supply weapons to Ukraine to frustrate Russia's geopolitical goals in the area. Russia does not intend to give up Ukraine to the West, Coffey and Gardiner contend, and Ukraine must grow its arsenal if it is to survive Russia's continued military support of the conflict there. Ultimately, the authors believe, the sending of American arms to Ukraine would show the world that international aggression such as Russia's will never go unpunished. Coffey is a fellow at the Margaret Thatcher Center for Freedom; Gardiner is director of the same organization.

As you read, consider the following questions:

1. What key areas of Ukraine do Coffey and Gardiner say Russia will attempt to capture to create a viable political entity in the country?

2. What defensive weapons do Coffey and Gardiner say would help Ukrainian forces determine the origins of artillery strikes?

3. What three consequences do Coffey and Gardiner say will affect the United States if it chooses not to act in Ukraine?

As Russian-backed forces make territorial gains in eastern Ukraine, and as a cease-fire agreement was reached in Minsk, Belarus, between Kyiv [the capital of Ukraine] and Moscow [the capital of Russia], there is intense debate in Washington about whether to send weapons to the Ukrainian military. There is no reason to believe that the cease-fire agreement will last when many such agreements have failed in the past. At this moment of crisis for Ukraine, the United States should be ready to help the people of Ukraine defend themselves by sending vital weapons and equipment if the government in Kyiv makes a request.

Any delivery of weapons to Ukraine must be part of a wider strategy led by Washington and its allies to rein in Russian ambitions in the region, including lifting restrictions on U.S. energy exports to Europe, withdrawing from the New Strategic Arms Reduction Treaty (New START), and strengthening the NATO [North Atlantic Treaty Organization] alliance to head off any potential threat by Moscow to the Baltic states and allies in Eastern and Central Europe.

Russia's Ambitions for Ukraine

There is nothing in Russia's recent past that leads one to believe it will stick to the cease-fire agreement. Almost seven years later, Russia still violates the 2008 cease-fire agreement with Georgia [that ended the Russo-Georgian War]. The cease-fire agreement last September in Ukraine only lasted a few weeks. Cease-fire or not, Russia's ultimate goal is to keep Ukraine out of the transatlantic community. In the short term, Russia will help the separatists consolidate gains in Donetsk and Luhansk in order to create a political entity that becomes more like a viable state. This will include the capture of important communication and transit nodes, such as the rail link at Debaltseve, Mariupol and its port, and the Luhansk power plant—all of which are under Ukrainian government control.

The separatists fighting in eastern Ukraine are Russian-backed, Russian-trained, and Russian-equipped. Soldiers kitted out in the latest military gear and wearing uniforms with Russian military insignias have been spotted. Military hardware such as T-72 tanks—which are not in the Ukrainian military's inventory—are being used in eastern Ukraine. In an era of prolific social media, this kind of major incursion can no longer be hidden from the outside world.

Why the Timing Is Right for Sending Arms

If the Ukrainian government makes a request for defensive weapons, there are three key reasons why now is the right time for the U.S. to comply:

1. Last year [2014] there was a slim hope that the conflict could be resolved peacefully. Now it is clear that Russia is only interested in escalating violence. The illusory peace sought by German chancellor Angela Merkel and French president François Hollande has merely bought Russia and the separatists more time. The idea that Moscow is committed to a peaceful resolution to the war in eastern Ukraine is fanciful. In fact, the only way out that Moscow sees is to defeat the Ukrainian military as quickly as possible, thereby compelling Kyiv to concede defeat.

2. In 2014, it was unclear in which direction Ukraine was heading. This is no longer the case. The Ukrainian people have demonstrated, whether on the streets of the Maidan [square] or through the ballot box, that they see their future in the West, not under Russian domination. As recently as one year ago, closer ties with the West were discouraged by Ukraine's leaders. Since the disposal of Russian-backed Ukrainian president Viktor Yanukovych last February this has all changed.

3. When Russia first started backing the separatists, the situation on the ground was chaotic. Nobody knew how far the separatists would go and when they would be stopped. The Ukrainian military was in disarray. Flooding the battlefield with advanced Western weaponry would have been dangerous. The situation is now different. There is a front line and a traditional linear battlefield. The Ukrainian military has been able to defend territory and in some cases retake land that was previously lost.

Which Weapons Should the United States Send to Ukraine?

The exact types of weapons needed are best determined by experts on the ground who have detailed knowledge of the local security situation, the capabilities of the Ukrainian military, and the capabilities of both the separatists and the Russian forces supporting their attacks. Generally speaking, the following defensive capabilities are urgently needed by the Ukrainian military:

- Anti-tank/armor weapons would be hugely beneficial, especially with the continued use of Russian T-72 tanks by the separatists.

- As the indiscriminate use of artillery and rockets increases, counter-battery radars are vital. They would allow Ukrainian forces to determine the origin of artillery strikes so they can respond quickly and accordingly.

- Secure communications equipment and unmanned aerial vehicles would significantly improve situational awareness on the battlefield and the coordination of effective military actions to counter separatist efforts.

A Broader Strategy Is Needed

Defensive weapons alone are not a panacea, but they can be an effective part of a larger strategy on the part of the West. Since Ukraine is not a NATO member it does not enjoy a security guarantee from the United States. However, the situation is not black and white: The alternative to direct U.S. military intervention is not to do nothing. In addition to providing defensive weapons, the U.S. can help Ukraine by:

- Expanding the target list of Russian officials under the Magnitsky Act [a 2012 US bill intended to punish Russian officials responsible for the death of Russian lawyer Sergei Magnitsky in a Moscow prison in 2009]. Washington should implement a greater range of targeted sanctions aimed directly at Russian officials responsible for violating Ukrainian sovereignty, including freezing financial assets and imposing visa bans.

- Developing a new diplomatic strategy for dealing with Russia. The U.S. could start by acknowledging that the Russian "reset" is—and has long been—dead. Russia has already been expelled from the G8 [a group of eight industrialized nations dealing with economic and political issues facing the global community], and NATO-Russia cooperation has been suspended. The U.S. should continue to marginalize Russia in other

Why the United States Should Intervene in Ukraine

So let's get right to why a Russian victory in Ukraine should matter to the West, and what we should be doing to make sure Kiev at least has a fighting chance.

As Russia's war against Ukraine transforms the military equation along Europe's periphery with breathtaking speed, the West continues to communicate that it will do nothing that would stop or at least complicate [Russian president Vladimir] Putin's military advance. If unchecked, Russian aggression may shift farther westward, this time into the NATO [North Atlantic Treaty Organization] area itself: the Baltics and, if the alliance continues to weaken and eventually unravels from the inside, possibly even into Poland and Romania.

Simply put, so long as NATO remains America's principal alliance and a means to project our power and influence, Ukraine is most emphatically our business. This is not about going to war; it's about extending military aid to a country under attack at a critical geostrategic point between Europe and Eurasia. Ukraine is our common problem as an alliance. This is about the growing threat of a wider war in Europe. It's time for Washington and its European allies to act accordingly.

Andrew A. Michta, "Why Ukraine Is Our Business,"
American Interest, *January 26, 2015.*

international fora, including the G20 [group of twenty central bank governors from twenty industrialized economies].

- Adopting a new global free-market energy policy. The U.S. should work immediately and comprehensively to eliminate barriers to U.S. energy exports. The benefits are obvious—reducing Europe's dependence on Russia to keep the lights on and the fires burning.

- Withdrawing from New START. New START is a fundamentally flawed treaty that dramatically undercuts the security of the United States and its allies. It does nothing at all to advance U.S. security, while handing Moscow a significant strategic edge in Europe. Russia's aggression in Ukraine jeopardizes the supreme interests of the United States, destabilizing a region crucial to the U.S. and the NATO alliance.

A Robust Message to Moscow

The West should arm the Ukrainians to give them a fighting chance to defend their homeland against external aggression. There are, of course, risks involved in providing military support, and Moscow will likely respond by further escalating its backing for the separatists. But the consequences of inaction are far greater, which would include the carving up of Ukraine, an emboldened Kremlin, and a weakening of American credibility on the world stage.

It is in the U.S. national interest for Ukraine to stave off Russia's invasion, and to reassert its territorial integrity. By sending arms to Ukraine, Washington will be sending Moscow a clear message that it cannot threaten its neighbors with impunity, and that there is a price to be paid for its blatant disregard for the principles of national sovereignty. Russian president Vladimir Putin's brutal and barbaric actions in Ukraine are unacceptable and must be met with strength and resolve by the free world.

> "[Sanctions] will send Putin a strong
> message that he can no longer get away
> with his efforts to destabilize Ukraine
> without significant consequences."

The United States Should Continue Imposing Sanctions on Russia

David J. Kramer

In the following viewpoint, David J. Kramer contends that the United States can curtail Russian violence against Ukraine by implementing new economic sanctions against Russia. Doing so, he believes, would show not only Russia but also the world that such breaches of any nation's sovereignty by an aggressor are unacceptable. Kramer also argues that strong American leadership on this issue could lead Europe to begin imposing harsher sanctions on Russia as well. Kramer is the president of Freedom House, a nongovernmental organization that advocates for democracy, political freedom, and human rights.

As you read, consider the following questions:

1. What steps does Kramer say Russian president Vladimir Putin took to suggest to the world that he was ready to end the Ukraine crisis?

2. What economic benefit does Kramer claim the United States will retain while imposing sanctions on Russia?

3. What three tactics does Kramer say Putin has been using to destabilize Ukraine?

President [Barack] Obama and his European counterparts can help end Russia's ongoing aggression against Ukraine by imposing new, tough sanctions against the regime of Vladimir Putin this week [in June 2014].

European heads of state meet Friday to decide whether to institute additional measures against Russia, but Obama should not wait another moment. He should announce immediately that the U.S. is going ahead with its own sanctions. American leadership might bolster the wobbly Europeans to take similar steps Friday, but even if it doesn't, it will send Putin a strong message that he can no longer get away with his efforts to destabilize Ukraine without significant consequences.

A Precarious Cease-fire

Putin this week launched a campaign to preempt decisions on sanctions by hinting at his readiness to end the Ukrainian crisis that he created. At his request, Russia's upper house of parliament, the Federation Council, revoked the authorization of military action that Putin requested in March. Putin also unenthusiastically endorsed Ukrainian president Petro Poroshenko's cease-fire offer and halfheartedly pressed the separatists he has supported in eastern Ukraine to accept it as well.

The move by the Federation Council is solely symbolic and can be undone at a moment's notice. As for the cease-fire, someone forgot to tell the Russian fighters in Ukraine, who shot down a Ukrainian helicopter on Tuesday, killing nine people. Sporadic fighting has continued in other parts of eastern Ukraine, prompting Poroshenko to threaten to end the cease-fire. Meanwhile, Putin visited Vienna where he pushed Austrian officials to agree to a new natural gas pipeline that would circumvent Ukraine, sowing further divisions in an already badly split Europe about how to handle Russia.

America's Opportunity

Putin's efforts may be paying off, as an unnamed European Union official on Tuesday predicted that the 28 European [Union (EU)] member states will not approve tougher measures on Friday. The Russian stock market and the value of the Russian ruble have risen this week to pre-crisis levels.

Obama has said he wants to maintain a united U.S.-EU position and to avoid unilateral sanctions. There is no question that a unified position of hard-hitting sanctions would be the preferred option. Given how badly divided the EU remains, however, such unity simply may be unachievable. . . .

Adding to Obama's reluctance to act unilaterally has been pressure from the American business community. "Unilateral sanctions by the United States end up with other countries and their industries filling the void," argued Linda Dempsey, vice president at the National Association of Manufacturers.

Yet such fears are overstated. Because of the extraterritorial nature of U.S. sanctions, foreign companies and banks would have to choose between doing business with Russian entities blacklisted by the U.S. and staying in the good graces of the U.S. Treasury Department. My bet is they will do the latter, given the recent case of BNP Paribas. One of France's largest banks, BNP Paribas this week tentatively agreed to a $9 billion settlement for violating U.S. economic sanctions by doing

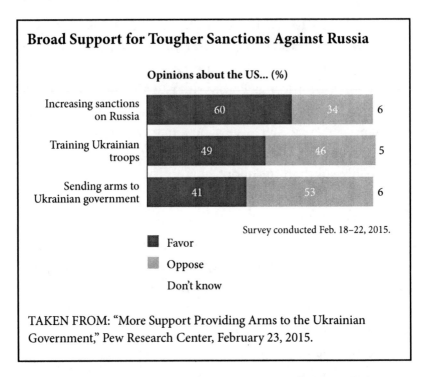

Broad Support for Tougher Sanctions Against Russia

Opinions about the US... (%)

	Favor	Oppose	Don't know
Increasing sanctions on Russia	60	34	6
Training Ukrainian troops	49	46	5
Sending arms to Ukrainian government	41	53	6

Survey conducted Feb. 18–22, 2015.

■ Favor
■ Oppose
Don't know

TAKEN FROM: "More Support Providing Arms to the Ukrainian Government," Pew Research Center, February 23, 2015.

business in Sudan, Iran, and Cuba; many of the banks' transactions in those sanctioned countries were routed through the U.S.

The sanctions already imposed against Russia by the U.S. have had impact, and given the fragile state of the Russian economy, a new round of measures could force Putin to back down in a serious way, not the phony way he has displayed in recent days.

Eliminating a Threat

Let's remember that the current crisis is the responsibility of Putin. Last fall, he pressured Ukraine's then president Viktor Yanukovych into abandoning deals with the European Union, setting off a wave of protests in Ukraine. In February, Putin offered Yanukovych a $15 billion bailout but only if Yanukovych brutally suppressed the protestors; more than 100 people were killed in downtown Kyiv. After Yanukovych fled Ukraine and forfeited power, Putin, terrified that such a scenario might be repeated in Russia, invaded Crimea and staged a rigged referendum that led to Russia's annexation of the peninsula in March.

For months, Putin has been doing his best to destabilize Ukraine by sending in forces and arms, including tanks, and cutting off energy supplies. More than 400 people have been killed in the fighting for the cause of separatism that few Ukrainians actually support. The so-called "separatist" leaders are in most cases Russian citizens; their frequent visits to Moscow for consultations underscore how easily the conflict could end should Putin decide—or be forced to decide—to do so.

This is no time to take Putin at his word. He remains a dangerous threat not only to Ukraine, but to all his neighbors and to European security and transatlantic stability. Obama must show U.S. leadership in confronting this threat through meaningful sanctions against Russian banks, energy firms, and defense and technology companies. Such leadership would advance U.S. national interests and might even prod the Europeans to follow suit and do the right thing, too.

> *"The United States will start rolling back sanctions on Russia only when the Minsk agreements are fully implemented."*

The United States Must Support the Minsk Agreement for Ukrainian Peace

Victoria Nuland

In the following viewpoint, Victoria Nuland contends that the international community must support the Minsk agreement to bring true peace to the embattled Ukraine. The agreement, she believes, will stop the war in eastern Ukraine, restoring government control over that region and allowing the Ukrainian people to begin rebuilding their country. The United States, Nuland contends, must stand by Ukraine in helping to implement this agreement. Nuland is assistant secretary of state for European and Eurasian affairs at the US Department of State.

As you read, consider the following questions:

1. In what areas of Ukraine's government does Nuland say the United States still needs to see reforms?

Victoria Nuland, Testimony on Ukraine before the Senate Foreign Relations Committee, US Department of State, March 10, 2015.

2. Which groups of people in Crimea does Nuland say are at risk of suffering human rights abuses under the new government?

3. In what parts of Ukraine does Nuland say the Ukrainian-Russian cease-fire is being violated?

Today Ukraine is central to our 25-year transatlantic quest for a "Europe whole, free and at peace." My interagency colleagues and I are pleased to update you [the Senate Foreign Relations Committee] today [March 10, 2015] on U.S. efforts to support Ukraine as it works to liberate the country from its corrupt, oligarchic past, chart a more democratic, European future, and bring an end to Russian-fueled violence. In my remarks, I'll focus on two areas: first, the work Ukraine is doing—with U.S. and international support—to reform the country, tackle corruption and strengthen democratic institutions; second, I will give an update on our efforts to support implementation of the February and September Minsk agreements, including our readiness to impose further costs on Russia if the commitments Moscow made are further violated. . . .

The Status of Ukraine

First—a quick reminder of why we're here. Sixteen months ago, the Kyiv Maidan [square] and towns across Ukraine erupted in peaceful protest by ordinary Ukrainians fed up with a sleazy, corrupt regime bent on cheating the people of their sovereign choice to associate with Europe. They braved frigid temperatures, brutal beatings and sniper bullets. The leader of that rotten regime fled the country, and he was voted out by the parliament—including most members of his own party. Then, Ukraine began to forge a new nation on its own terms—signing an Association Agreement with the European Union; holding free and fair elections—twice—even as fighting raged in the east; and undertaking deep and comprehensive economic and political reforms.

Against the backdrop of Russia's aggression, the situation in the country remains precarious. Ukraine's leaders, in the executive branch and the parliament, know they are in a race against time to clean up the country and enact the difficult and socially painful reforms required to kick-start the economy, and meet their commitments to their people, the IMF [International Monetary Fund] and the international community. The package of reforms already put forward by the government, and enacted by the Rada [Verkhovna Rada of Ukraine, the parliament of Ukraine], is impressive in its scope and political courage.

Just last week:

- They passed budget reform expected to slash the deficit this year, and strengthen decentralization by giving more fiscal control to local communities;

- They made tough choices to reduce and cap pension benefits, increase work requirements and phase in a higher retirement age;

- They created a new banking provision to stiffen penalties for financiers for stripping assets from banks at the public's expense, a common practice among oligarchs;

- And, they passed laws cutting wasteful gas subsidies and closing the space for corrupt middlemen that buy low, sell high and rip off the Ukrainian people. These laws will also enhance corporate efficiency, incentivize domestic production, and use $400 million in increased revenue from state-owned gas companies to help care for the poor, including some of the 1.7 million people driven from their homes by the conflict.

With U.S. support—including a $1 billion loan guarantee last year and $355 million in foreign assistance and technical advisors—the Ukrainian government is:

- helping insulate vulnerable Ukrainians from the impact of necessary economic reforms;

- improving energy efficiency in homes and factories with metering, consumer incentives and infrastructure improvement;

- building e-governance platforms to make procurement transparent and basic government services cleaner and publicly accessible;

- putting a newly trained force of beat cops on the streets of Kyiv who will protect, not shake down, the citizens;

- reforming the prosecutor general's office (PGO)—supported by U.S. law enforcement and criminal justice advisors—and helping energize law enforcement and just prosecutions;

- moving to bring economic activity out of the shadows;

- supporting new agriculture laws—with the help of USAID [United States Agency for International Development] experts—to deregulate the sector and allow family farms to sell their produce in local, regional and wholesale markets; and

- helping those forced to flee Donetsk and Luhansk with USAID jobs and skills training programs in places like Kharkiv.

And there's more support on the way. The president's budget includes an FY16 [fiscal year 2016] request of $513.5 million—almost six times more than our FY14 request—to build on these efforts.

The Work Ahead

To turn the page, Ukraine's hard work must continue. Between now and the summer, we must see budget discipline maintained and tax collection enforced across the country—notably including on some of Ukraine's richest citizens who have enjoyed impunity for too long. We need to see continued reforms at Naftogaz [the national gas and oil company of Ukraine] and across the energy sector; final passage of agriculture legislation; full and impartial implementation of anti-corruption measures, including a commitment to break the oligarchic, kleptocratic culture that has decimated the country.

As I said in my last appearance before this committee, the most lasting antidote to Russian aggression and malign influence in the medium term is for Ukraine to succeed as a democratic, free market state and to beat back the corruption, dependence and external pressure that have thwarted Ukrainians' aspirations for decades. For this to happen, we must ensure that the government lives up to its promises to the Ukrainian people, and keeps the trust of the international financial community. And, at the same time, the United States, Europe and the international community must keep faith with Ukraine, and help insure that Russia's aggression and meddling can't crash Ukraine's spirit, its will or its economy before reforms take hold.

Which brings me to my second point—even as Ukraine is building a peaceful, democratic, independent nation across 93% of its territory, Crimea and parts of eastern Ukraine are suffering a reign of terror. Today Crimea remains under illegal occupation, and human rights abuses are the norm, not the exception, for many at-risk groups there—Crimean Tatars, Ukrainians who won't surrender their passports, journalists, LGBT [lesbian, gay, bisexual, and transgender] citizens and others.

In eastern Ukraine, Russia and its separatist puppets unleashed unspeakable violence and pillage. This manufactured conflict—controlled by the Kremlin [the Russian government]; fueled by Russian tanks and heavy weapons; financed at Russian taxpayers' expense—has cost the lives of more than 6000

Ukrainians, but also of hundreds of young Russians sent to fight and die there by the Kremlin, in a war their government denies. When they come home in zinc coffins—"Cargo 200," the Russian euphemism for war dead—their mothers, wives and children are told not to ask too many questions or raise a fuss if they want to see any death benefits.

Western Solidarity

Throughout this conflict, the United States and the EU [European Union] have worked in lockstep to impose successive rounds of tough sanctions—including sectoral sanctions—on Russia and its separatist cronies as the costs for their actions. In Crimea, we have shown through our investment sanctions that if you bite off a piece of another country, it will dry up in your mouth. Our unity with Europe remains the cornerstone of our policy toward this crisis.

And it is in that spirit that we salute the efforts of German chancellor [Angela] Merkel and French president [François] Hollande in Minsk [the capital of Belarus] on February 12th to try again to end the fighting in Ukraine's east. The Minsk package of agreements—September 5th, September 19th and the February 12th implementing agreement—offer a real opportunity for peace, disarmament, political normalization and decentralization in eastern Ukraine, and the return of Ukrainian state sovereignty and control of its territory and borders. Russia agreed to it; Ukraine agreed to it; the separatists agreed to it. And the international community stands behind it.

For some eastern Ukrainians, conditions have begun to improve. Along long areas of the line of contact, particularly in Luhansk Oblast, the cease-fire has taken hold; the guns have quieted in some towns and villages; some weapons have been withdrawn; some hostages have been released.

But the picture is very mixed. Since the February 15th cease-fire, the OSCE [Organization for Security and Cooperation in Europe] Special Monitoring Mission has recorded hundreds of violations. Debaltseve, a key rail hub beyond the cease-fire lines, fell to the separatists and Russian forces six days after Minsk was signed and three days after the cease-fire was to come into effect. In Shchastya, in villages near the Donetsk airport, in Shyrokyne and other towns around Mariupol the shelling continues, as verified by OSCE special monitor authority.

A Brighter Future?

In the coming days, not weeks or months—here is what we need to see:

- A complete cease-fire in all parts of eastern Ukraine;

- Full, unfettered access to the whole conflict zone including all separatist-held territory, for OSCE monitors; and

- A full pullback of all heavy weapons—Ukrainian, Russian and separatist—as stipulated in the agreements, under OSCE monitoring and verification.

If fully implemented, this will bring greater peace and security in eastern Ukraine for the first time in almost a year. And with it, Ukraine will once again have unfettered access to its own people in the east, and the opportunity for dialogue and political normalization with them. That's what Minsk promises. Peace, then political normalization, then a return of the border. But first, there must be peace.

Russia's commitments under the Minsk agreements are crystal clear and again the choice is Russia's. As the president has said, we'll judge Russia by its actions, not its words. The United States will start rolling back sanctions on Russia only when the Minsk agreements are fully implemented.

But the reverse is also true. We have already begun consultations with our European partners on further sanctions pressure should Russia continue fueling the fire in the east or other parts of Ukraine, fail to implement Minsk or grab more land as we saw in Debaltseve.

Mr. Chairman, members of this committee, America's investment in Ukraine is about far more than protecting the choice of a single European country. It's about protecting the rules-based system across Europe and globally. It's about saying "no" to borders changed by force, and to big countries intimidating their neighbors or demanding spheres of influence. It's about protecting our 25-year American investment in the prospect of a Europe whole, free and at peace, and the example that sets for nations and people around the world who want more democratic, prosperous futures.

> *"If the Minsk agreement is all but guar-*
> *anteed to fail, has anything been*
> *achieved at all? The short answer is,*
> *not very much."*

Ukraine's Minsk Agreement Will Not Bring Peace

Alexander Mercouris

In the following viewpoint, Alexander Mercouris contends that the Minsk agreement between Ukraine and Russia will not end the war in eastern Ukraine. In Mercouris's view, this is due to Ukraine's unwillingness to follow the agreement's stipulations, as the country's president has refused to negotiate with Russian-backed separatist leaders. As a result, Mercouris claims, the deal is pointless, and the war will likely continue. Mercouris is a lawyer and writer on international affairs.

As you read, consider the following questions:

1. What does Mercouris say was the good result of the Normandy, France, meeting between Russian president Vladimir Putin and Ukrainian president Petro Poroshenko?

2. According to Mercouris, what are the ways in which Ukraine's government reneged on the initial Minsk protocol?

3. What does Mercouris suggest as the only way for Ukraine to end its ongoing war with Russia?

The new Minsk agreement is almost certainly unenforceable and is very unlikely to lead to a political settlement that will end the war.

Its significance is that it provides more evidence of the pressure [German chancellor Angela] Merkel is under and shows that the balance of political advantage is shifting towards the Russians.

However it is not a breakthrough and the war will almost certainly continue.

The Political Context

To understand what happened in Minsk, it is necessary to discuss the diplomatic background.

A popular uprising began in the Donbass [a region in eastern Ukraine] in April 2014, shortly after the February coup that brought the Maidan movement [referring to the Euromaidan movement, a wave of demonstrations and civil unrest in Ukraine that began in November 2013 with public protests in Kiev demanding closer European integration] to power. In its initial stages, the uprising was peaceful and its demands moderate.

These were for a political democratisation of the region, which had up to then been tightly controlled from Kiev, which appointed its governors.

The new Maidan government refused to negotiate with the leaders of the uprising, branding them instead "terrorists" in the pay of Russia. It launched what it called an "anti-terrorist operation" ("ATO") to destroy them.

This steadily escalated over the course of the spring and summer, until on 30th June 2014 it evolved into a full-scale military assault on the Donbass by the Ukrainian army backed by right-wing volunteer militias and the Ukrainian air force.

The Russians responded by launching a diplomatic initiative to settle the conflict by peaceful means. The idea was that there should be negotiations between the Donbass and the Maidan government in Kiev to settle the conflict through a new constitution that would take into account the Donbass's aspirations.

The concept was for a federal structure, loosening Kiev's formerly tight political control of the Donbass. This proposal for what has become known as "federalisation" was first floated in discussions between the Russians and the Germans in the days immediately following the February coup.

The Constitution Situation

The question of a new constitution had actually been placed on the agenda in the weeks before the Maidan coup. Its supporters at that time were the Maidan leaders, who pressed the idea on [Viktor] Yanukovych. The 21st February 2014 agreement, brokered by the EU [European Union] and signed by Yanukovych and the Maidan leaders, envisaged a national unity government and negotiations on a new constitution to be completed before the end of 2014.

In the event the coup took place the following day, the 21st February 2014 agreement was repudiated by the Maidan leaders, a proper national unity government was never formed and the negotiations to agree a new constitution never took place. Since the coup, the Maidan leaders have turned from being supporters of the idea of a new constitution to its bitter opponents.

On 17th April 2014 a statement was agreed in Geneva between Russia, Ukraine, the US and EU, that alongside various steps to calm the conflict (including a repudiation of the use of force to settle it) called for an "inclusive national dialogue" to settle the question of Ukraine's constitution. The precise words were

> "The announced constitutional process will be inclusive, transparent and accountable. It will include the immediate establishment of a broad national dialogue, with outreach to all of Ukraine's regions and political constituencies, and allow for the consideration of public comments and proposed amendments."

Though it signed the Geneva statement, the Maidan government made no effort to implement it by starting such a dialogue. Instead it launched the ATO.

Russian diplomatic efforts nonetheless continued. On 4th June 2014 [Russian president Vladimir] Putin met [Petro] Poroshenko, Ukraine's newly elected president, during the D-Day commemorations in Normandy. Poroshenko informed Putin that he had a peace plan to settle the conflict.

Poroshenko's "peace plan", when published on 20th June 2014, turned out to be nothing of the sort. Though making a token concession in paragraph 11 to "decentralisation" and referring in passing to a new constitution, no procedure to achieve this was set out.

The Cease-fire Proposal

The plan was largely made up of demands amounting to an ultimatum for the unconditional surrender of the uprising in 7 days.

A declaration on 2nd July 2014 made in Berlin by the foreign ministers of Germany, France, Ukraine and Russia calling for swift action to enforce a cease-fire was disregarded. Instead a decision made by Ukraine's security council on 30th June 2014 to launch a general military offensive to crush the uprising was implemented causing the conflict to escalate into full-scale war.

The Normandy meeting between Putin and Poroshenko on 4th June 2014 did bear one fruit in the form of the setting up of a contact group of Russia, Ukraine and the Organization for Security and Co-operation in Europe ("OSCE") whose purpose is supposedly to implement Poroshenko's peace plan.

The contact group has become the key instrument in all subsequent diplomatic negotiations. The Minsk protocol of 5th September 2014 and the Minsk agreement of 12th February 2015 are its products, being in theory amendments to Poroshenko's peace plan. . . .

In Russia, Putin and his government are far more likely to be criticised for the moderation and restraint they have shown throughout this conflict than for the supposed "aggressiveness" and "expansionism" the West constantly talks about.

The diplomacy since the start of the uprising in the Donbass in April 2014 nonetheless shows that it is Russia that has consistently sought a peaceful settlement of the conflict through negotiations and that it is the Maidan government in Kiev which has consistently chosen war. I have previously discussed here on RI [Russia-Insider.com] why the Maidan government left to itself will always choose [war] rather than compromise.

Desperate to avoid total disaster, Poroshenko in September appeared to agree a peace deal, the basic outlines of which were laid out by Putin supposedly during a flight to Ulan Bator [the capital of Mongolia]. The exact terms were hammered out on 5th September 2014 by the contact group, this time with the participation of the leaders of the Donbass, and were set out in a document known as the Minsk protocol.

Failing Negotiations

The Minsk protocol spelt out a political process whereby the Donbass would hold elections and be granted special status pending constitutional negotiations that would finally settle its status. This is of course in line with Russian ideas that the conflict should be settled by the parties themselves through negotiations.

The Maidan government reneged on the Minsk protocol. It failed to agree the terms of the elections in the Donbass. It rescinded the law of special status the Minsk protocol required it to grant. It took no step towards the constitutional negotiations that would determine the Donbass's future.

Instead the Maidan government refused to recognise the elections the Donbass held in November 2014, imposed an economic blockade on the Donbass and refused to observe the terms of a cease-fire also agreed on 5th September 2014 by failing to withdraw from territory it had agreed to hand over and by refusing to withdraw its heavy weapons from the conflict zone.

Despite a drastically deteriorating economic situation, it instead rearmed and reinforced its army in the Donbass in preparation for a new offensive, which it launched at the end of January 2015.

That offensive has ended in disaster, with heavy loss of life, the loss to the militia of Donetsk airport and the encirclement by the militia of 5–8,000 Ukrainian troops in the town of Debaltseve.

It is this disaster that has set the stage for the negotiations that took place in Minsk on 11th and 12th February 2015.

These negotiations represent a departure from the negotiations that have gone before.

All previous negotiations were initiated by the Russians. These latest negotiations were not initiated by the Russians. On the contrary, they have been giving signs recently that they have given up on negotiations. . . .

The negotiations were initiated by Angela Merkel most probably with the support of more moderate or "realist" elements within the US government, who flagged up their intentions in an editorial in the *New York Times* that I have previously discussed. . . .

Ukrainian Difficulties

The result is the frantic negotiations we have seen over the last few days. The key meeting was the one Merkel and [French president François] Hollande held with Putin in Moscow on Friday 6th February 2015.

I have discussed the dynamics of the negotiations, with the Russians negotiating from a position of advantage as a result of the defeats the Ukrainians have suffered on the battlefield.

The result is that we now have another contact group statement and a four-power declaration that reflects long-standing Russian ideas. Whilst there are similarities with the Minsk protocol of 5th September 2014, the details are more fully spelt out and for the first time since the February coup a time line has been agreed.

There is agreement on a cease-fire and the withdrawal of heavy weapons from the Donbass. The economic blockade Kiev has imposed on the Donbass is supposed to be lifted. The Ukraine is supposed to pass a law of special status for the Donbass before the end of March. Elections in the Donbass are then supposed to take place, this time supervised by the OSCE so as to prevent Ukraine from disputing their legality and outcome.

All this is supposed to pave the way for the constitutional negotiations the Russians have always insisted on, which are supposed to produce results before the end of the year.

In return, the Russians are supposed to restore control of the border to whatever authority is created in Kiev as a result of the constitutional negotiations.

The obvious problem with this agreement, as with every other agreement the Maidan movement has ever made since

Minsk Agreement Will Not End Fighting

An end to the fighting and killing in eastern Ukraine would certainly be a gratifying result [of the Minsk agreement]. But in view of the details that have since been announced about the current agreement, skepticism would seem to be more than justified. For if the package of measures that has now been agreed is examined more closely, it becomes apparent that this new deal—Minsk II—does not go much further than the first Minsk agreement, which was struck back in September 2014. There, too, a cease-fire and the withdrawal of heavy weapons were agreed upon, but the truce never really held.

The Russian-backed fighters have now won territory on several fronts through military offensives. The focus of fighting at present is the important railway hub of Debaltseve, which the separatists have allegedly surrounded, but which Ukrainian government troops understandably do not want to yield without a fight. As the cease-fire is not scheduled to begin for a good two days, it can't be ruled out that the clashes around Debaltseve won't grow in intensity over the next few hours, as both sides try to gain a military advantage before the truce goes into force.

But there are other reasons for considerable skepticism as to whether the truce agreed for February 15 [2015] will really be kept. For, in the end, no truce agreement has any chance of success unless the demilitarized zone between the warring parties is adequately monitored and enforced by independent forces.

Ingo Mannteufel, "Opinion: Minsk II Leaves Many Questions Unanswered," Deutsche Welle, February 12, 2015.

the start of the Maidan protests in November 2013, is that the Maidan movement is not going to abide by it.

That this is so is shown by Poroshenko's behaviour in Minsk. Not only did he refuse to allow any reference to the word "federalisation" to appear in any of the documents produced at the meeting even as a possible outcome of the constitutional negotiations (a fact which in itself has no significance), but far more importantly he categorically refused to meet the Donbass leaders or negotiate with them directly and threatened to leave the meeting when called on to do so. He even refused to sign the Minsk agreement, leaving it to his representative on the contact group, Leonid Kuchma, to sign it in his place.

This makes it a virtual certainty that this agreement will fall by the wayside as every other agreement has done. It is doubtful whether it will even lead to an interruption of the fighting, which seems if anything to be intensifying.

The only thing that might make the agreement stick is if Merkel forces Poroshenko and the Ukrainian government to abide by it. This is not something she has been prepared to do up to now. The political imperative that forced her to initiate the latest round of negotiations might in theory oblige her to do so. However that would require her to face down the hardliners in the US and Europe, which she has never up to now been prepared to do.

A Bleak Future

Beyond that, there is the further problem that Merkel's personal relationship with Putin is in tatters. She has been forced to agree to what Putin has been demanding all along. For someone used to getting her way, that must be humiliating.

Putin for his part would not be human if he were not furious with some of the things Merkel has been saying about him over the last few months, in particular her calling him a liar. The grim faces and poor personal chemistry between the two were obvious from the photographs of the meetings in Moscow and Minsk and do not promise well for future cooperation between the two to make the Minsk agreement stick.

If the Minsk agreement is all but guaranteed to fail, has anything been achieved at all? The short answer is, not very much. The Russians have managed to move the focus further in their direction by putting the question of constitutional negotiations at centre stage and by linking the question of control of the border to the successful outcome of these negotiations.

That does force acceptance of the Russians' idea that some form of autonomy for the Donbass is the only way out of the crisis, putting more pressure on Kiev to grant it. The Russians are certain to bring this up in the future, when more negotiations take place.

The negotiations have also exposed an element of division between the Germans on the one hand and the US and EU hard-liners on the other, a fact confirmed by the angry articles complaining of "appeasement" that have appeared in parts of the British press today [in February 2015]. However, unless Merkel is prepared to take far more decisive steps than she has up to now, talk of a rift is exaggerated and it would be unwise to make too much of this.

A pessimistic but realistic view is that this conflict is still at a relatively early stage. The risk of escalation remains high. Unless Merkel surprises by taking a much stronger line with Poroshenko than past experience suggests she will, the overwhelming probability remains that these negotiations will be remembered as a footnote to a conflict that will be decided not at the negotiating table but on the battlefield.

Periodical and Internet Sources Bibliography

The following articles have been selected to supplement the diverse views presented in this chapter.

Doug Bandow	"Ukraine Fight Flares Again: U.S. Should Keep Arms and Troops at Home," *Forbes*, May 11, 2015.
Rob Garver	"If the U.S. Arms Ukraine, Russia Vows Retaliation," *Fiscal Times*, February 10, 2015.
Paul R. Gregory	"'Ukraine Is Fighting Our Battle,'" *Hoover Digest*, Fall 2014.
Adrian Karatnycky	"Making the Most of Minsk," *New York Times*, February 20, 2015.
Marina Kortunova	"Russia: US Involvement in Ukraine Adds Fuel to Fire," PressTV, April 25, 2015.
Aliaksandr Kudrytski and Ryan Chilcote	"Belarus Leader Urges U.S. Involvement in Ukraine Peace Process," Bloomberg Business, March 31, 2015.
Jeff Mankoff	"U.S. Should Keep Force as Option for Ukraine," CNN, February 27, 2015.
Ukraine Today	"Minsk Agreement: Ukraine Peace Deal Terms in English," February 12, 2015.
Carol J. Williams	"U.S. Faces Quandary: Will Sending Arms to Ukraine Help or Do Harm?," *Los Angeles Times*, February 10, 2015.
Kevin Zeese	"Chomsky and Kissinger: Don't Increase US Military Involvement in Ukraine," AlterNet, February 5, 2015.

OPPOSING
VIEWPOINTS®
SERIES

CHAPTER 2

Should the West Intervene in Ukraine?

Chapter Preface

In February and March of 2014, Ukrainian president Viktor Yanukovych abdicated his office after an angry Ukrainian populace began protesting his decision to direct Ukraine toward further economic integration with Russia rather than with Western Europe. With the country in upheaval, the Ukrainian parliament elected a new, democratic government to lead the country into closer association with the West, which, for Ukrainians, bore the promise of economic prosperity and modernity.

Russia responded to these developments with hostility, as it viewed the presence of a Western-friendly country on its border, especially one it had once dominated as the Soviet Union, as a threat to its national security. Russia eventually invaded Ukraine and annexed its peninsula territory of Crimea. A civil war subsequently broke out between the new Ukrainian government's military and Russian-supported separatists in Ukraine's southern and eastern regions.

While all of this was occurring in Ukraine, Western Europe was hosting its own disagreements on the subject. The two main questions being debated throughout Ukraine's political troubles were whether Ukraine should join the European Union (EU)—the political and economic partnership of twenty-eight European countries—and the North Atlantic Treaty Organization (NATO), the military alliance between numerous European nations as well as Canada and the United States.

Although the European Union was founded in 1993, the idea of a politically and economically integrated Europe dates to the postwar world of the 1950s. At this time, the nations of Europe determined that they should work to prevent indefinitely the kind of widespread violence and destruction brought upon them by World War II. Therefore, in 1957, Belgium,

France, West Germany, Italy, Luxembourg, and the Netherlands together signed the Treaty of Rome, which established the European Economic Community (EEC). This meant that all six founding countries would now share one trade market and customs union.

The European Union itself was founded in 1993 by the Maastricht Treaty. While retaining the transnational economic benefits of the EEC, the EU introduced some additional advantages for member states: all members would now use one currency, the euro, while sharing policies on foreign relations, security, and immigration, all with the aim of promoting peace and prosperity across Europe.

Membership in the EU means that countries enjoy the benefits of collective economic stability and trade. However, the criteria for retaining membership in the EU require nations to host strong democratic governments and free market economies. These two issues came to light amid the Ukraine crisis in 2014 and 2015. Ukraine itself claimed it could meet its financial obligations for EU membership in several years, while detractors warned that Ukraine's economy was in such tatters that admitting the country to the EU would destroy economies across the continent.

The prospect of Ukraine's joining NATO was slightly more controversial. The military alliance was formed in 1949 chiefly as a deterrent against potential aggression by the Communist Soviet Union. The stipulations of the North Atlantic Treaty that created NATO stated that all members were obligated to defend any other member that was attacked by an outside power. When the Soviet Union fell in 1991, NATO continued on as a North American/European watchdog alliance, working to prevent the rise of the type of nationalism and militarism that had sparked both World War I and II.

Today Russia views NATO as a perpetual threat to its existence, as the country is the reason NATO was originally founded. This is the reason Russia vehemently opposes NATO membership for Ukraine, for if Ukraine were ever to join the alliance, the combined armies of Europe and North America could become present on Russia's border at any time. In 2014 Russian prime minister Dmitry Medvedev stated that Russia would consider a Ukraine joined with NATO to be a military enemy.

The following chapter presents opposing viewpoints concerning Ukraine's relationship with Western Europe. The topics covered include the questions of potential Western intervention in the Ukraine crisis, whether the European Union should integrate Ukraine, and whether NATO should actively defend Ukraine from Russian-supported forces in Ukraine's civil war.

| "The West must focus . . . on targeted assistance to the Ukrainian military that strengthens its capacity and effectiveness in the long term."

The West Should Help Ukraine

Ian Kearns, Steve Andreasen, and Des Browne

In the following viewpoint, Ian Kearns, Steve Andreasen, and Des Browne argue that the West should intervene in the Ukraine crisis to strengthen both its military and economy. Not to do so would destroy relations between Eastern and Western Europe as well as show Russia that its aggression is acceptable behavior, the authors write. Ultimately, the authors claim, the West needs to implement long-term democratic reforms in Ukraine to help it survive as the strong, free nation it wants to be. Kearns is the director of the European Leadership Network. Andreasen is a national security consultant at the Nuclear Threat Initiative. Browne is chair of the European Leadership Network.

As you read, consider the following questions:

1. What four areas do the authors claim the West should address in a broader effort to help Ukraine?

2. What do the authors identify as the inefficiencies of Western economic sanctions in trying to stop Russia?

3. How do the authors claim Russian president Vladimir Putin would interpret Western refusal to strengthen Ukraine's military?

The uncertain implementation of the fragile Minsk II cease-fire agreement in eastern Ukraine has paused the debate in the United States and Europe over whether or not to provide the Ukrainian military with "defensive lethal assistance." That debate will almost certainly pick up steam again, in particular if Ukrainian separatists supported by Russia continue to attack the Ukrainian armed forces in and around Debaltseve in violation of Minsk II. Yet, even if defensive lethal assistance as now envisioned could be rushed to the Ukrainian battlefield and used effectively by the Ukrainian armed forces, it is unlikely to deliver a change to the strategic military balance on the ground in the short term, and hence in part is a dangerous distraction. What is needed now is a much broader effort to address Ukraine's short-term economic crisis, support its political and economic reform, tackle corruption, and reform its police and judiciary. That effort should definitely include long-term support for Ukraine to modernise, equip, professionalize and make fully democratically accountable its military and security institutions.

Lesser Alternatives

The arguments against arming Ukraine now with defensive lethal assistance, including light anti-armour missiles, have been well rehearsed. Simply stated, it is difficult to imagine the scale of assistance suggested by some in the US being sufficient to deter Russia from continuing its support for the Ukrainian separatists and their current efforts to draw a more coherent and defensible political and military line in the separatist eastern regions. And while it may be unlikely that such military assistance would be sufficient to trigger new Russian-backed military offensives that otherwise had been unintended, there is a more than negligible risk that Russia could respond by escalating the conflict even further.

The policy implication of this sobering conclusion is that Chancellor [Angela] Merkel [of Germany], President [François] Hollande [of France] and President [Petro] Poroshenko [of Ukraine] were right to pursue a diplomatic solution that has some chance of effectively "freezing" the conflict in eastern Ukraine and stopping the killing. The looming problem for the West, however, relates to what comes next in Ukraine, no matter how effective the implementation of the Minsk II agreement is over the next 10 months.

One point should now be clear: sanctions by themselves do not amount to a comprehensive strategic response to what is going on. Several recent independent assessments of Western sanctions on the Russian economy concur that the most likely impact is of prolonged stagnation. This will hurt many in Russia but may not impact Russian decision making or help Ukraine. Moreover, the option of further strengthening sanctions to the extent that they would have a greater impact on the Russian economy may not be a viable option, not least because there is great nervousness (in many European capitals) at the consequences of what would effectively be an attempt to turn Russia into a nuclear armed failed state. The increased economic damage such a policy would do to the rest of Europe is also at the forefront of policy makers' minds.

The Wrong Solution

However, if one imagines a scenario in which the West both refuses to arm Ukraine and sanctions fail to modify Russian

Looking Ahead for Ukraine

Ukraine has not yet died—as the country's anthem observes. . . .

I have no idea what will happen in Ukraine tomorrow, let alone next week. But I know what all Europeans should want to happen over the next year and the next decades. In February 2015, on the 70th anniversary of the Yalta [Conference] agreement, Ukraine should again be a halfway functioning state. A corrupt and rackety one but still the kind of state that, in the long run, forges a nation. It should have signed an Association Agreement with the EU [European Union] but also have close ties with Russia. In February 2045, on the 100th anniversary of the Yalta agreement, it should be a liberal democratic, rule-of-law state that is a member of the EU but has a special relationship with a democratic Russia. "Pie in the sky!" you may say. But if you don't know where you want to go, all roads are equally good. This is where we should want to go.

That outcome would obviously be good for Ukraine. Less obviously, it would be good for Europe. Look at the shifting balance of world power, and look at the demographic projections for Western Europe's ageing population. We'll need those young Ukrainians sooner than you think, if we are to pay our pensions, maintain economic growth and defend our way of life in a post-Western world. . . .

Worse than ridiculous is the notion that the EU should not intervene in any way because this is a purely Ukrainian affair.

Timothy Garton Ash, "Ukraine Stands on the Brink—and Europe Must Bring It Back," Guardian, February 2, 2014.

policy towards de-escalation and a political resolution of the conflict, then the West will be perilously close to accepting an outcome with profoundly negative consequences not only for Ukraine but for the entire system of international relations in Europe.

It is one thing to say that attempts to rush defensive lethal assistance to help Ukraine fight a war with Russia in the weeks and months ahead are unlikely to deliver the advertised strategic effect. It is quite another to say that Ukraine should not receive any support to modernise and strengthen its military, period, or until a comprehensive settlement of all issues with Russia is reached.

The latter position gives President [Vladimir] Putin [of Russia] a veto over Ukraine's legal and moral right to defend itself. In the context of a demonstrated Western unwillingness, for very good reason, to fight a war with Russia in the Eastern part of Ukraine, he could read it as a green light to intimidate other governments in the region as he sees fit. Amid all the Western talk that there can be no privileged spheres of influence, this would be tantamount to conceding him one.

Tangible Support

To avoid this outcome, the West must focus not so much on emergency defensive lethal aid for use on today's battlefield, but on targeted assistance to the Ukrainian military that strengthens its capacity and effectiveness in the long term. The Ukrainian military also needs to be embedded in a web of democratically accountable institutions that are loyal to, and provide the physical security for, the future economic and political development of Ukraine and its people. This long-term support needs to focus on the training of Ukrainian military personnel and on providing them with effective and secure command, control and communication facilities.

The recent announcement by a senior US military official that the US will send troops to train three battalions of Ukrai-

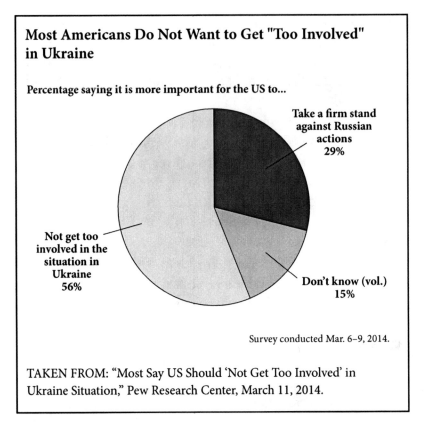

Most Americans Do Not Want to Get "Too Involved" in Ukraine

Percentage saying it is more important for the US to...

Take a firm stand against Russian actions
29%

Not get too involved in the situation in Ukraine
56%

Don't know (vol.)
15%

Survey conducted Mar. 6–9, 2014.

TAKEN FROM: "Most Say US Should 'Not Get Too Involved' in Ukraine Situation," Pew Research Center, March 11, 2014.

nians from the Interior Ministry at the Yavariv training center in the western Ukrainian city of Lviv is a useful start. Provision of further training and non-lethal materiel support from other NATO countries and partners should also be encouraged. Ukraine can be helped to buy the weapons systems it needs on the open market from many countries, including those outside NATO, if need be. It can also be helped to manufacture at least some of what it needs domestically.

None of this assistance will work however, if it is carried out as a quick fix or in the absence of the wider reform that Ukraine needs. In the end, as President [Sauli] Niinistö of Finland said in little noticed comments at the Munich Security Conference on 7th February, if Ukraine can build a democratic, stable, prosperous and socially just state and society that all of its citizens value and wish to defend, it is this, more than anything else, that will be the best long-term guarantee of its security.

"It is time for the EU and Russia to put mutual recriminations aside and work together to prevent the collapse of the Ukrainian economy."

Europe Should Integrate Ukraine

Nicolai Petro

In the following viewpoint, Nicolai Petro argues that Western Europe should integrate Ukraine so that the country can exist peacefully as a member of both Eastern and Western Europe. To do this, however, Petro writes, Europe must respect Ukraine's cultural identity and not treat it simply as any other European nation. Petro believes that if Europe accepts Ukraine, it could simultaneously integrate Russia, which would benefit the entire European economy. Petro is professor of political science at the University of Rhode Island.

As you read, consider the following questions:

1. What does Petro identify as the root of Russia's and Ukraine's failure to join with the rest of Europe?

Nicolai Petro, "How the E.U. Can Bring Ukraine into Europe," opednews.com, January 18, 2014. © 2014 OpEdNews.com. All rights reserved. Reproduced with permission.

2. According to Petro, why have Western European leaders historically avoided engaging in meaningful dialogue with Eastern Europe?

3. For what three purposes does Petro say Ukraine would need as much as $60 billion?

The situation in Ukraine is a problem for all Europeans, whether they live within the EU [European Union] or outside it. It stems from the fact that there is at present no cultural context that allows all Ukrainians to feel at home in Europe. Ukraine's westernmost regions, which once belonged to the Austro-Hungarian Empire and Poland, can use this as a peg upon which to hang their European identity. But in the rest of the nation, which has long been attached to Russia, people are alienated by efforts to force Ukraine to choose between the EU and Russia. And when they see how Russia is constantly berated by European leaders for trying to strengthen ties with Ukraine, they wonder how their own distinctive values and culture will be treated by the EU.

Identity Crises

Sadly, the EU's Association Agreement with Ukraine offers them no answers. There is nothing in it that addresses Ukraine's cultural and historical distinctiveness or that acknowledges its deep historical, cultural, and economic ties with Russia. Nor does it suggest that Ukraine's Slavic and Orthodox heritage will have any role to play in shaping contemporary European values. It is merely a set of conditions that one part of Europe has set for the other part. The reward is, ostensibly, a more prosperous life. The cost is your soul.

The solution to Ukraine's malaise is obvious, and it lies with Russia. Were Russia to be acknowledged as an essential part of Europe, and its incorporation become part of the EU's strategic vision, Ukraine's identity crisis would all but disappear. The whole of Ukraine could simply be what it already is—part of both Eastern and Western Europe.

Instead of embracing a Russia in Europe, however, the EU chose exclusion. The Eastern Partnership initiative was set up at the behest of Poland and Sweden after the 2008 crisis in the Caucasus to tear several former Soviet states away from Russia's "sphere of influence" and bring them into Europe's. This targeted omission of Russia made the entire project highly divisive in all six nations invited to participate. As a result only two, Moldova and Georgia, have gone through even the first stages of association.

The roots of this failure lie, first and foremost, in the EU's reluctance to engage with Russia and Ukraine in a dialogue of equals. Such a dialogue must involve a serious, perhaps even at times contentious, discussion of the values gap that has emerged between the more secularized and liberal European West and the more conservative and religious European East.

A Necessary Partnership

Western European leaders have shied away from such a dialogue because it would move beyond the familiar routine of lecturing the neighbors on the appropriate liberal values and force them to address Eastern European concerns about the moral and ethical course of modern European society. It is far easier to mouth the mantra of an insurmountable "values gap" than it is to try to resolve these differences in a constructive manner.

The Ukraine is a case in point. Its current dilemma is that, while it cannot join the Russia-led Customs Union because of the political ramifications, it also cannot afford association with the EU because of the economic costs. Current EU mechanisms are simply inadequate to the task of supporting such a costly economic transition. Ukraine's problems demand a much larger and more comprehensive program of

Aid to Ukraine Would Create Stronger Europe

Some have argued that little has changed in Ukraine since the Maidan "Revolution of Dignity" last year [2014] except for the faces of those who make up Ukraine's political establishment. But the opposite is true: In stark contrast to life before Maidan, Ukraine's leaders are now working hard for the good of our country. . . .

Most important, we have clearly defined our priorities, which include a commitment to a democratic state and European integration. Ukrainians championed such ideas during the Maidan protests and reaffirmed them in last year's presidential and parliamentary elections. The most ambitious goal set in [Petro] Poroshenko's "Ukraine 2020" reform program is that Ukraine should be ready to apply for the European Union [E.U.] membership in five to six years. We wish to counter the myth of Russian propaganda that Europe is not interested in pursuing E.U. membership for Ukraine. . . .

Aid to Ukraine is an investment in a safer, stronger and wealthier Europe. While defensive military aid would help make Ukraine a secure frontier of the Western world, financial and political assistance are crucial to the success of reforms that would create a burgeoning market of more than 40 million people. As the financier George Soros has argued recently, the European Union could trigger greater economic growth for itself by helping to forge a stable and Europe-oriented Ukraine. . . .

It is time to marshal all of the energy and resources necessary to reform Ukraine—not just for Ukrainians but also for a free and strong Europe.

Borys Lozhkin, "More Aid to Ukraine Would Invest in a Stronger Europe," Washington Post, January 26, 2015.

support. Such a program, in fact, would require the combined resources of both the Customs Union and the EU.

Last month Russia did its part by reducing gas prices for Ukraine by one-third and offering to buy $15 billion in Ukrainian Eurobonds. But that will not be nearly enough. By next summer Ukraine may need as much as $60 billion to pay for public services, repay part of its IMF [International Monetary Fund] debt, and service various private loans and other interest payments.

It is time for the EU and Russia to put mutual recriminations aside and work together to prevent the collapse of the Ukrainian economy. Stepping up to the plate with a package of financial assistance comparable to Russia's would go a long way toward addressing one of the main Ukrainian criticisms of the current agreement; i.e., that the EU is simply indifferent to the economic impact that such a massive transition would have on the lives of millions of people.

A European Union

The EU leadership, however, continues to insist that the European Union and the Customs Union (and its eventual successor the Eurasian Union) are incompatible institutions, even though as late as last September European Commissioner Štefan Füle suggested that the issue ultimately boiled down to a difference in tariff levels (see Samuel Charap and Mikhail Troitskiy, "Russia, the West and the Integration Dilemma," *Survival*, December 2013–January 2014). The EU's obstinacy on this point is hard to understand since the Customs Union was designed to adopt many EU standards in order to make possible an eventual merger with it. A joint approach to the economic difficulties that affect the entire continent therefore makes eminent sense.

But as important as the benefits for Ukraine would be, there would be many broader benefits of such a joint effort. Instead of constantly getting bogged down in debates over which side was more successful at snatching portions of the common European home away from the other, this issue, if handled as a common European challenge, could provide a practical and positive mechanism for involving Russia in European affairs. If there must be competition in post–Cold War Europe, let it be for who can contribute the most to a more stable and prosperous Europe.

The economic collapse of Ukraine need not happen. It is an avoidable catastrophe, if all parties can work together. The EU should therefore be encouraging Ukraine, Russia, and indeed all the former Soviet states, to become equal partners in building Europe's future. As former German foreign minister Hans-Dietrich Genscher once put it: "Man braucht sich!" ("We need each other!")

> *"By joining the Association Agreement with Ukraine, the European Union does not get a new market for exports but rather a big black hole."*

Europe Should Not Integrate Ukraine

Alexander Donetsky

In the following viewpoint, Alexander Donetsky argues that the European integration of Ukraine would spell economic disaster for both parties. Ukrainians would become bankrupt and poor due to price increases, Donetsky writes, while Europe would lose money when Ukraine consumes products for which it cannot pay. According to Donetsky, those who push for European-Ukrainian integration do so for their own political ends. Donetsky is a contributor to the Strategic Culture Foundation.

As you read, consider the following questions:

1. Which three political entities does Donetsky say encouraged Ukraine to seek integration with Europe?

2. What does Donetsky say would result in Ukraine once the country ended its economic and military cooperation with Russia?

3. What two branches of the Ukrainian economy does Donetsky say would face difficult transitions once integrated into Europe?

Up to the autumn of 2013, very few Ukrainian politicians had been acquainted with the text of the EU [European Union]-Ukraine Association Agreement. The content had not even been openly accessible in Ukrainian or Russian languages, and people could not read it. The only thing they had patience for was going through the short text of the basic agreement itself without multiple amendments containing the most scandalous provisions. With the amendments the document exceeded 900 pages.

The Wrong Reasons

The publications highlighting the details appeared in February–March 2013, sparking a real row. The implementation of the agreement would have made Ukraine collapse, entailing impoverishment of population. In September the scandal started to rage, making the leadership read the document and make an independent study of possible consequences. No matter the strong pressure on the part of the United States, Ukraine did not sign the document at the Eastern Partnership summit held in Vilnius [capital of Lithuania]. The February coup brought to power the people fully controlled by the United States. They intend to sign the economic part of the agreement on June 27 [2014]. This is a political decision taken under pressure that does not take into account the interest of Ukraine.

Anyone who followed the events related to the Vilnius summit knows it was not the "old Europe" who pushed Ukraine into this direction but rather the United States, Poland and Lithuania. Poland has a clear interest: the introduction of European norms would allow over 80 thousand Poles [to] demand restitution of the property expropriated after Western Ukraine joined the Union of Soviet Socialist Republics.

Lithuanian president [Dalia] Grybauskaite wants the summit to be a success, opening the way for her promotion to a top position within the framework of the European Union structure, something she aspires to.

The United States is pursuing its geopolitical interests.

The West in Ukraine

First, the EU-Ukraine Association Agreement means putting an end to Ukraine's economic and military cooperation with Russia to weaken the latter's military potential. Ukraine would refuse common standards and customs levies would come into life.

Second, the agreement makes Ukraine part of [an] all-European system of security based on NATO [North Atlantic Treaty Organization], where the United States plays the leading role. Actually it becomes an issue of moving US military presence to Russia's borders.

Third, the agreement provides American companies access to Ukrainian arable land and mineral resources. US agricultural giants specializing on genetically modified products are getting ready to start business in Ukraine. Burisma, a private oil and gas company in Ukraine, has appointed Hunter Biden, the youngest son of US vice president Joe Biden, to its board of directors. The younger Mr. Biden isn't the only American with political ties to have recently joined Burisma's board. Devon Archer, a former senior advisor to current secretary of state John Kerry's 2004 presidential campaign and a college roommate of Mr. Kerry's stepson H.J. Heinz, signed on in April. Mr. Biden and Mr. Archer are also managing partners at Rosemont Seneca Partners, a Washington, DC–based invest-

ment company. Former president of Poland Alexander Kwaśniewski is also a member of Burisma's board of directors. Naturally it raises serious conflict-of-interest questions for Western countries' Ukraine policy.

Hard Times

Fourth, joining the agreement would lead to negative consequences for common Ukrainians, things like impoverishment, bankruptcy of middle and small business enterprises, hikes of household costs resulting in migration. The flows of immigrants will rush to Russia. Waves of people leaving Poland would hit Europe too. It would exacerbate the problem of unemployment, inevitably giving rise to ethnic crime.

Fifth, Europe and Russia will have to spend time and effort to deal with [a] humanitarian disaster near their borders. It will sap their resources, limiting options for tackling other burning problems.

Sixth, some branches of [the] Ukrainian economy integrated into Europe (metallurgy and chemicals produced by some Ukrainian oligarchs) will face difficulties of [a] transition period to make them curtail the production. At first glance, it would meet the interests of Europe, doing away with competitors. But Ukrainian high-tech enterprises operate in Europe, not in Ukraine. It's the European Union they pay taxes to. If taxes are not paid it hurts the European Union, not the United States.

A Careful Decision

Nobody took seriously the possibility of competition on the part of Ukraine while the agreement was in [the] works. They talked about saturating Ukraine with high-quality European goods. Actually, it was about creating a new market for European producers. Perhaps it would have been so a couple of years ago but the 2013 crisis substantially brought the Ukrainians' living standards down. After the February coup, the Nazi government launched a number of economic experiments and started a war with its own people; the situation has deteriorated to the extent that people cannot satisfy elemental basic needs anymore.

According to HeadHunter, 54% [of] males and 58% [of] females cannot pull on till the next time they get their salary; the time is coming when people will not be able to make ends meet. Today Ukraine is considered at immediate risk of defaulting on its foreign debt that amounts to around 40% of annual gross domestic product. The tearing up [of] economic ties with Russia will deliver a severe blow. The Russian Federation consumes one-third of Ukrainian exports. By joining the Association Agreement with Ukraine, the European Union does not get a new market for exports but rather a big black hole, sucking in European commodities without paying for what it consumes. If there is no profit made, then how will it affect the European Union's economy? This [is] a rhetorical question; the deal with Ukraine can inflict enormous damage.

All told, one should say that this is the time for prudence. The new Ukrainian rulers have shown they are ready to eliminate their own country while serving the US interests. If the European Union leaders recklessly succumb to political ambitions and outside pressure, they'll fall into a trap, having to face a grave threat. True, the United States is the leading lobbyist pushing the EU-Ukraine Association Agreement through. But does it serve the interests of Europe and the common people?

> "As Ukraine shows, far from keeping the
> peace, NATO is a threat to it."

NATO Should Not Become Involved in Ukraine

Seumas Milne

In the following viewpoint, Seumas Milne contends that members of the North Atlantic Treaty Organization (NATO) should not intervene to save Ukraine from Russia because it was NATO that created the conflict. The military alliance's expansion into Eastern Europe, Milne claims, is what originally caused Russia to occupy Ukraine and protect itself from a European army on its border. To create peace in Ukraine, Milne believes, NATO must stop expanding eastward while attempting to intervene in the affairs of other nations. Milne is a British journalist and contributor to South Africa's Mail & Guardian *newspaper.*

As you read, consider the following questions:

1. According to Milne, how did Ukrainian prime minister Arseniy Yatsenyuk describe Russia in relation to the Ukraine crisis?

2. What three cases does Milne cite as examples of NATO's status as the advance guard of an American new world order?

3. Which Ukrainian political party does Milne say the national government is attempting to ban from future elections?

For the West's masters of war, it's a good time to be in Wales. A military alliance that has struggled for years to explain why it still exists has a packed agenda for its Newport summit.

The North Atlantic Treaty Organisation (NATO) may not be at the centre of Barack Obama and David Cameron's [prime minister of the United Kingdom] plans to ramp up intervention in the Middle East and wipe ISIS [Islamic State in Iraq and Syria; also known as the Islamic State in Iraq and the Levant, or ISIL] "out of existence". But after 13 years of bloody occupation of Afghanistan and a calamitous intervention in Libya, the Western alliance at last has an enemy that seems to fit its bill.

The NATO Problem

Swinging through the former Soviet republic of Estonia this week, the US president declared that NATO was ready to defend Europe from "Russian aggression".

NATO's secretary general, Anders Fogh Rasmussen—who insisted as Danish prime minister in 2003 that "Iraq has weapons of mass destruction . . . we know"—has released satellite images supposed to demonstrate that Russia has invaded Ukraine. Not to be outdone, the British prime minister has compared Vladimir Putin with Hitler.

The summit is planning a rapid reaction force to be deployed across Eastern Europe to deter Moscow. Britain is sending troops to Ukraine for exercises. In Washington, Congress hawks are demanding action to give Ukraine "a more capable fighting force to resist" Russia.

Any hope that talk of a cease-fire agreement by Ukraine's president might signal an end to the conflict was sunk when his prime minister, Arseniy Yatsenyuk, described Russia as a "terrorist state" and, encouraged by Rasmussen, demanded that Ukraine be allowed to join NATO.

It was precisely the threat that Ukraine would be drawn into a military alliance hostile to Russia, despite the opposition of most Ukrainians and its then elected government, that triggered this crisis in the first place.

Mistakes of the Past

NATO has been the cause of escalating tension and war, which is how it's been since it was founded in 1949, at the height of the Cold War, six years before the Warsaw Pact, supposedly as a defensive treaty against a Soviet threat. It's often claimed the alliance maintained peace in Europe for 40 years, when in fact there is not the slightest evidence the Soviet Union ever intended to attack.

After the USSR [Union of Soviet Socialist Republics] collapsed, the Warsaw Pact was duly dissolved. But NATO was not, despite having lost the ostensible reason for its existence. If peace had been the aim, a collective security arrangement including Russia, under the auspices of the United Nations, could have been formed.

Instead, it gave itself a new "out of area" mandate to wage unilateral war, from Yugoslavia to Afghanistan and Libya, as the advance guard of a US-dominated new world order. In Europe it laid the ground for war in Ukraine by breaking a US pledge to Moscow and relentlessly expanding eastwards: first into ex–Warsaw Pact states, then into the former Soviet Union itself.

But the "biggest prize", as the head of US-funded National Endowment for Democracy put it last year, was ethnically di-

End Ukrainian Civil War by Ending International Meddling

The best thing for Ukraine is to force NATO [North Atlantic Treaty Organization], the US, and regional players out of the country, former US congressman and presidential candidate Ron Paul said. Without foreign meddling in the civil war, Kiev will focus on the nation's economic collapse.

"Get the foreigners out of there [Ukraine], get the Europeans out, the US out, get NATO out, and get the Russians out," Paul said at the International Students for Liberty Conference in Washington on Friday [February 13, 2015]. *"There will be less of a civil war going on there because they will have to worry about their debt. This is an economic matter too. You have to realize that the country is totally bankrupt."* . . .

Paul—a 79-year-old retired doctor who spent nearly three decades in the US Congress representing the state of Texas—reiterated his previous statements, noting that what happened in Ukraine last year was a *"coup"* that was planned by *"NATO, EU [European Union]"* and western Ukrainians. *"One thing for sure that we do know, is we [US] had the conversations between our State Department and our ambassador before the coup—who will we put in place. And they planned part of the coup."* . . .

Russian president Vladimir Putin recently criticized NATO's involvement in the Ukrainian conflict, claiming the Ukrainian army is essentially a *"NATO legion"* which fails to *"pursue the national interests of Ukraine"* and is interested in restricting Russia.

"'Get NATO, Foreign Countries Out of Ukraine to End Civil War'–Ron Paul," RT, February 16, 2015.

vided Ukraine. After the European Union made its military-linked Association Agreement with Ukraine, exclusive of a Russian deal—and Ukraine's corrupt but elected president, who refused to sign it, was overthrown in a US-backed coup by any other name—it was hardly paranoid for Russia to see the takeover of the neighbouring state as a threat to its core interests.

Out of Control

Six months on, Moscow-backed eastern Ukrainian resistance to the NATO-backed nationalists in Kiev has become full-scale war. Thousands have died and human rights abuses have multiplied on both sides, as government troops and their irregular auxiliaries bombard civilian areas and abduct, detain and torture suspected separatists on a mass scale.

The Ukrainian forces backed by Western governments include groups such as the neo-Nazi Azov Battalion, whose symbol is the wartime Nazi stormtroopers' wolf's hook. The increasingly repressive Kiev regime is now attempting to ban the Ukrainian Communist Party, which won 13% of the vote at the last parliamentary elections.

But then NATO, whose members have often included fascist governments in the past, has never been too fussy about democracy. Evidence for its claims that Russian troops have invaded eastern Ukraine is also thin on the ground. Arms supplies and covert intervention in support of the Donbass rebels [referring to the Donbass People's Militia, part of the United Armed Forces of Novorossiya and considered a terrorist group in Ukraine] including special forces and state-backed irregulars are another matter.

This is what NATO powers such as the US, Britain and France have been busy doing all over the world for years, from Nicaragua to Syria and Somalia. The idea that Russia has invented a new form of "hybrid warfare" in Ukraine is bizarre.

That's not to say the proxy war between NATO and Russia in Ukraine isn't ugly and dangerous. But it's not necessary to have any sympathy for Putin's oligarchic authoritarianism to recognise that NATO and the EU [European Union], not Russia, sparked this crisis—and that it's the Western powers that are resisting the negotiated settlement that is the only way out, for fear of appearing weak.

That settlement will have to include federal autonomy, equal rights for minorities and military neutrality as a minimum: in other words, no NATO.

NATO likes to see itself as the international community. In reality it's an interventionist and expansionist military club of rich-world states and their satellites used to enforce Western strategic and economic interests. As Ukraine shows, far from keeping the peace, NATO is a threat to it.

"NATO leaders need to make some tough decisions and push back militarily against Russia."

NATO Should Confront Russia over Ukraine

Kurt Volker and Erik Brattberg

In the following viewpoint, Kurt Volker and Erik Brattberg argue that the North Atlantic Treaty Organization (NATO), to uphold its duty of defending Europe, must intervene in Ukraine against Russia. This, according to the authors, would show Russia that aggressive actions against sovereign countries always incur penalties. In this way, the authors believe, NATO could assist in building a united, peaceful continent. Volker is a former US ambassador to NATO and the executive director of the McCain Institute for International Leadership, where Brattberg is a visiting fellow.

As you read, consider the following questions:

1. What two other non–NATO members besides Ukraine do the authors name as possible future targets of Russian president Vladimir Putin's aggression?

2. What specific aspects of direct military and intelligence support do the authors suggest NATO provide to Ukraine?

3. What four nations do the authors claim should be invited to join NATO immediately?

Vladimir Putin is placing a cynical bet that he can invade Ukraine just one week before a NATO [North Atlantic Treat Organization] summit—and that NATO will do nothing to stop him. The alliance must prove him wrong.

Despite sharp words from Brussels, Washington, London and Berlin, the Russian president believes that NATO lacks the will to challenge his dismemberment of Ukraine. By sending troops, tanks and artillery directly into the Ukrainian fighting, Putin is making a point: He will fight for Ukraine, and NATO will not. He is calling NATO's bluff.

The Western response will be read carefully from Kiev to Tallinn to Moscow. For the sake of Ukraine's integrity as a country, for future European security and for NATO's credibility as a defense organization, NATO leaders need to make some tough decisions and push back militarily against Russia.

NATO's Sacred Defense

NATO has already taken significant, positive military steps concerning its members in the east—particularly Poland, the Baltic states and Romania. This is important: The alliance's only obligation is to collective defense. That must be sacrosanct.

NATO has increased air policing over the Baltics, expanded exercises, promised to strengthen its defense planning and decided to deploy ground forces temporarily in Eastern Europe. These strong steps will cause Russia to think twice before expanding its aggression from Ukraine to NATO member states.

However, drawing such a bright line around NATO territory is being read by Putin as a signal that non-members such as Ukraine, Georgia and Moldova are—literally—up for grabs. With Russia's invasion of eastern Ukraine in the open, NATO needs to focus not only on defending alliance members but also on crisis management and projecting power beyond NATO territory.

Friends and Enemies

To prove Putin wrong, NATO should take the following steps at its Wales summit:

—Provide direct military and intelligence support to the Ukrainian government. This means advisers, trainers, equipment and the possibility of direct reinforcement using NATO air and ground capabilities. Anti-tank weapons and air-defense systems should be in the mix. The most critical need is tactical: helping Ukraine use its own equipment and troops to reestablish a border with Russia, isolate separatists and avoid firefights to the greatest extent possible.

—Cancel all allied sales of military and dual-use equipment to Russia. The most notorious case is the French naval assault vessels—*Mistral* and *Sebastopol*—but other allies, including Britain and Germany, have yet to scrap all of their sales to Russia. As for the French ships: NATO should buy them for itself using its infrastructure budget and deploy them as a naval component to the NATO Response Force.

Economics and Security

—Impose further sanctions—including on Gazprom [Russian natural gas company] and its leadership. Russia believes it has the upper hand in deterring strong Western action by threatening energy supplies. Europe needs to call Russia's bluff, showing that it can survive an energy showdown better than Russia can. The United States and Europe should also give a renewed push to European energy security efforts—including speeding delivery of U.S. liquefied natural gas (LNG) to Europe, and establishing a joint U.S.-E.U. [European Union] financing mechanism to spur completion of LNG terminals and pipeline interconnectors.

—Establish a multinational NATO military presence on the territory of Poland and the Baltic states. NATO secretary general Anders Fogh Rasmussen said this week that such action may be taken. It is critical that NATO prevent expansion of Russian aggression—and the best deterrence is preventive deployment. Any complaints that such a step violates the 1997 NATO-Russia Founding Act are negated by the first clause of NATO's undertaking: "In the current and foreseeable security environment." Russia's actions have fundamentally changed the security environment foreseen in 1997.

—Reaffirm NATO's commitment to building a Europe whole and free and at peace. Montenegro is ready for NATO membership now. Macedonia should be invited based on an urgent resolution of the dispute regarding its name. Finland and Sweden should be told they are welcome any time. And NATO should renew its pledge to work with Ukraine, Georgia and other partners on reforms necessary to help them qualify for membership. NATO must not accept a Russian diktat over the affairs of neighboring states.

Although it did not start out this way, the upcoming summit in Wales may be the most important NATO gathering since Prague in 2002, when NATO added seven members. The signal the organization sends next week—whether it will stand up for European security or concede to Russian aggression—will ripple through Europe for years to come.

Periodical and Internet Sources Bibliography

The following articles have been selected to supplement the diverse views presented in this chapter.

Australian	"The West Has to Confront Putin," February 23, 2015.
Roger Boyes	"Arming Ukraine Will Stop Putin in His Tracks," *Times* (London), February 4, 2015.
Roger Cohen	"Western Illusions over Ukraine," *New York Times*, February 10, 2015.
Economist	"Ukraine, Russia and the West: The Long Game," September 6, 2014.
Mark N. Katz	"Russia, Ukraine and the West," Eurozine, May 6, 2015.
Daniel Larison	"The West and Ukraine," *American Conservative*, January 20, 2015.
Alexander J. Motyl	"The West Should Arm Ukraine: Here's Why—and How," *Foreign Affairs*, February 10, 2015.
North Atlantic Treaty Organization	"NATO's Relations with Ukraine," October 1, 2015.
Matthew Parris	"It's Time We Washed Our Hands of Ukraine," *Times* (London), February 28, 2015.
Steven Pifer	"Russian Aggression Against Ukraine and the West's Policy Response," Brookings Institution, March 4, 2015.
Elizabeth Pond	"Russia vs the West: The Consequences of Putin's Invasion of Ukraine," *New Statesman*, March 5, 2015.

What Should Be Russia's Place in Ukraine?

Chapter Preface

The Ukraine crisis that began largely with Russia's 2014 occupation and annexation of Ukraine's Crimea region generated a wealth of opinions from both sides of the political divide. Supporters of Ukraine argued that Russia had acted aggressively by invading a sovereign country and stealing its land. Pro-Russia writers, meanwhile, justified Russia's acquisition of Crimea by arguing that most Crimean citizens were ethnic Russians and that the region itself, along with Ukraine, had historically belonged to Russia. An intimate political and cultural relationship exists between Ukraine and Russia, these commentators believed, one that could not possibly be understood by Westerners who claimed Russia had simply bullied Ukraine and appropriated its territory.

The intertwined histories of Ukraine and Russia began in the ninth century AD, when Scandinavian Vikings invaded Eastern Europe and founded Kievan Rus, the first East Slavic empire. The Slavic word "Rus" was used by Eastern Europeans to refer to the red hair of the Vikings. Kievan Rus extended from the Baltic Sea of Scandinavia to the Black Sea in southeastern Europe. The empire was centered in the capital of Kiev, the present-day capital of Ukraine.

Kievan Rus ruled in Europe for four hundred years, but in the thirteenth century, it was almost completely overrun and destroyed by the invading Mongol Empire. The last vestiges of Kievan Rus power were then forced north to a rustic imperial outpost known as Moscow. Meanwhile, the former Rus capital of Kiev was fought over and claimed by numerous local powers. Following Ukraine's invasion by the Mongols, the area was occupied by Poland and Lithuania, which ruled Ukraine for several hundred years. By the eighteenth century, however, the Russian Empire on Ukraine's eastern and northeastern border had risen to great power. In the late 1700s, Russia took Ukraine for itself, calling its new prize "little Russia."

The Russian Empire ruled Ukraine into the early 1900s, all the while suppressing rising Ukrainian patriotism by, for example, prohibiting children from speaking their native Ukrainian in school. When the Russian Empire fell in 1917, Ukraine finally declared itself an independent nation, with Kiev as its capital. In 1918, however, both Poland and the new Bolshevik government in Russia invaded Ukraine and fought each other for control of the country. The Bolsheviks eventually triumphed, and Ukraine was forcibly drawn into the Soviet Union in 1922.

The relationship was not harmonious. In the early 1930s, Soviet leader Joseph Stalin ordered a famine among Ukrainian farmers as retaliation for rejecting the Soviet institution of collective farms. About ten million Ukrainians died as a result. World War II brought further hardship to the country. Many Ukrainians allied themselves with the invading Nazis, believing they would free them from Soviet oppression. However, the Nazis eventually enslaved the Ukrainian people, and millions of Ukrainians subsequently joined the Soviet Union's Red Army to crush the German invaders. After the war, Stalin had thousands of Ukrainians who had collaborated with Germany either imprisoned or executed.

Ukraine remained a Soviet possession until 1991, when the Soviet Union fell and was replaced by the Russian Federation, a constitutional republic. After acquiring its independence, Ukraine established itself as a Western-style democracy but still could not escape the watchful eye of its former dominator. Into the 2000s, many Ukrainians accused Russia of interfering in Ukrainian politics by rigging elections and inserting Russian cronies into Ukrainian office. One such alleged leader was Viktor Yanukovych, who was elected president of Ukraine in 2010 but forced from power three years later for attempting to bring Ukraine back under Russian influence.

Ukraine then elected a new government in the hopes of becoming a pure democracy and allying itself with the West, free from Russian corruption and interference.

The following chapter presents numerous viewpoints on the Ukraine crisis and the country's current relationship with Russia.

| "The crisis in Ukraine owes far more to
| Western meddling than Russian."

The West Is Responsible for Provoking Russia over Ukraine

Tim Black

In the following viewpoint, Tim Black argues that the Ukraine crisis was caused by Western interference in Ukraine's political affairs and not by Russian military aggression. Europe has been trying to provoke Russia by offering Ukraine membership in the European Union and the North Atlantic Treaty Organization (NATO), Black writes, and both of these scenarios threaten Russian national security. A peaceful diplomatic solution, Black believes, is ultimately best for alleviating Ukraine's turmoil. Black is deputy editor of Spiked *magazine.*

As you read, consider the following questions:

1. What does Black claim Russia saw happen in Ukraine that made it invade Crimea?

2. What two American presidential administrations does Black blame for attempting to make Ukraine an enemy of Russia?

Tim Black, "How the West Drove Russia into Ukraine," *Spiked*, September 1, 2014. Copyright © 2014 Spiked Ltd. All rights reserved. Reproduced with permission.

3. What three Western offenses does Black blame for the protests that drove the Ukrainian president from office?

The mainstream story of the conflict in Ukraine is mind-meltingly simple: It was Russia wot dunnit. Since the fall of its [Ukraine's] Russian puppet of a president, Viktor Yanukovych, Russia has ceaselessly and relentlessly pursued a policy of military aggression against Ukraine. It really is that simple. Everything that is happening in Ukraine, from the displacement of nearly 300,000 people, to the killing of 2,200 more, is the fault of Russia and its chest-beating throwback of a president, Vladimir Putin.

Western Delusion

Just listen to what Western politicians are saying. US president Barack Obama's administration has talked darkly of Russia's 'pattern of escalating aggression'; Republican senator John McCain has spoken explicitly of the Russian 'invasion' as the work of 'an old KGB colonel [who] wants to restore the Russian empire'; and German foreign minister Frank-Walter Steinmeier admitted at the weekend [in August 2014] that thanks to Russia's 'border infringements', 'the situation is slipping out of control'. Little wonder that the *Times* editorial talks in concerned tones of 'Mr Putin's war'. Because that's what it looks like: a war planned out and pursued by Putin.

And why might Putin be waging this massively costly, de-stabilising war? Because, so the story goes, he and his cronies want to create a new Russian empire. This is clearly what one *Guardian* columnist has in mind when he writes that Putin has 'a long-term plan to recreate a greater Russia by regaining control of Ukraine and other states in the "near abroad."' According to a US academic in the *Globe and Mail*, it's all part of Putin's 'dream of imperial restoration', his 'delusionary imperial ambitions'. And why the additional adjective 'delusionary'? Because the key character in this brilliantly simple story of Russian aggression, Putin, is also undeniably mad. Why else would he be trying to act out his imperial dreams, runs the logic, if he didn't have a screw loose? 'Mr Putin is not rational', states a *New York Times* op-ed: 'Any rational leader would have reeled from the cost of Western sanctions.' *Slate* goes further: '[Putin's] actions are certainly consistent with the portrait of an enraged, hypernationalist, conspiratorial madman who is heedless of the consequences to Russia and to himself.'

So there you have it. The situation in Ukraine is the product of the machinations of the Moscow madman, and his circle of ex-KGB macho men. It is Russia's fault. The bloodshed in Ukraine, its fragmentation, its region-shaking instability—all of it can be laid at Russia's feet.

The True Story

Or at least it could be if any of this were true. Yes, Russia did annex Crimea, a region of Ukraine with a mainly ethnically Russian population. Yes, there clearly are Russian soldiers operating in eastern Ukraine (reports estimate 1,000). And, yes, the pro-Russian separatists in places like Donetsk will have had support from Russia. But none of this is the result of Putin's 'dream of imperial restoration', or his 'hypernationalist, conspiratorial madness'. Russia is not realising any sort of premeditated plan at all. In fact, it is not determining events; it is responding to them.

It saw anti-Russian protesters in Kiev violently replace Ukraine's democratically elected leader, Yanukovych, with a pro-Western government complete with a faction of bona fide neo-fascists in February. And it watched on as Western leaders serenaded Ukraine's new government with songs of approval. And seeing what happened, seeing Ukraine transformed into a strategic threat right on its own borders, Russia responded by swiftly taking back Crimea, and then attempted to shore up other parts of eastern Ukraine. Russia's intervention in

Ukraine isn't madness; it's a rational, realist response to what it correctly perceives as a geopolitical threat right there in its own backyard.

In fact, as we have consistently argued on *Spiked*, the crisis in Ukraine owes far more to Western meddling than Russian. In fact, for the past 20 years, Western leaders have thoughtlessly, blunderingly provoked and frightened Russia over Ukraine. They have tried to pull Ukraine into the orbit of the EU [European Union], if not the EU itself. They have issued the half-baked offer of NATO [North Atlantic Treaty Organization] membership to Ukraine, while simultaneously withdrawing it. And they have persistently, and self-aggrandisingly, talked of 'promoting democracy' in Ukraine and promulgating 'Western values'. And what has made this so dangerous, what has led the region to the precipice, is that those selfsame Western actors pushing this policy-triad in the Ukraine don't even recognise their intervention, their meddling, their clueless interference in Russia's neighbour and onetime ally, for what it is: a provocation and a threat to Russia.

But that is precisely what it must appear as to Russian eyes. From Bill Clinton's US administration of the mid-1990s pushing for NATO expansion (which led to the incorporation of such eastern bloc stalwarts as Bulgaria, Hungary, Romania and Latvia between 1999 and 2004), to the [George W.] Bush administration's 2008 half-promise to Georgia and Ukraine that they 'will become members of NATO', Western leaders have long looked set on turning Ukraine into a military adversary of Russia. Then there's the EU's march eastwards, with its 2008 initiative, the Eastern Partnership scheme, designed to integrate Ukraine into the European economy. And to ice these two layers of a distinctly Western cake to be served out on Russian borders, there has been the constant drum of pro-democracy rhetoric from the West, in which Ukraine is posited as an eastern outpost ripe for transformation into a Western-style liberal democracy. Indeed, US assistant secretary of state Victoria Nuland has admitted that since 1991, the US has spent upwards of $5 billion on pro-democracy initiatives in Ukraine.

A History of Interference

What happened at the end of last year [2013], when anti-Russian, pro-EU demonstrators converged on Maidan square in Kiev, and eventually drove the elected president from office, was not the beginning of Ukraine's current conflict. Rather, those protests were fuelled by years of Western interference in the region, years of 'pro-democracy' propaganda, and years of economic/military promises. Given the West's semi-unwitting role in fermenting the unrest, it is unsurprising that Western leaders blithely endorsed the protests and celebrated the downfall of Yanukovych. This, after all, was what they had long wanted.

That is why then German foreign minister Guido Wester-welle thought nothing at the time of announcing that 'the hearts of the people of Ukraine beat for the EU'. This is why Senator McCain happily undertook a backslapping tour of the protest camps in December, before declaring, 'We are here to support your just cause'. This is why then UK foreign secretary William Hague unthinkingly praised Ukraine's anti-government protesters: 'It is inspiring to see these people standing up for their vision of the future of Ukraine: a free, sovereign, democratic country with much closer ties to the European Union.' It was the culmination of a years-long, blundering, blustering attempt to turn Ukraine Western. Not because it served a particular geopolitical purpose, but because it just seemed right. And with little really at stake in Ukraine, why not? All this righteous posturing certainly plays well to a domestic audience.

Now, tragically, the reason why not is painfully clear. A whole nation is being torn asunder as Russia desperately tries to manage the chaos the West has unleashed on its borders.

This is not to endorse Russia's response; its interventions are understandable, but they're not helpful. Its continued military incursions are acting as a block to the one possibly useful and peaceful solution—a federal solution within Ukraine itself.

Be that as it may, there's no doubt where the finger of blame should really be pointing as Ukraine continues to unravel. And that is to those Western leaders who continue to provoke Russia. And what makes this all the more dangerous is that they do so blindly, with little sense of geopolitics or strategic interests—indeed, with little sense of the real stuff of international politics. They continue to talk of Ukraine's NATO membership; they continue to pull what's left of Ukraine's economy towards the EU; and they continue ever more shrilly to counterpose Western values, and Western progressiveness, to the dark un-PC [not politically correct] traditionalism of their imagined Russia. And on top of that, they continue to paint Russia as the aggressor, as the source of all Ukraine's problems.

Russia's military involvement in Ukraine is dangerous; but more dangerous still are the Western drivers of regional instability who time and again intervene with no sense of consequence and no sense of responsibility.

"We—that is, the West—are not responsible for Putin's behaviour."

The West Has a Choice: Abandon Ukraine or Punish Russia? It Should Choose the Latter

Alex Massie

In the following viewpoint, Alex Massie contends that Russia alone caused the Ukraine crisis by invading Crimea and violating Ukraine's sovereign rights. The West, Massie believes, cannot be blamed for its history of trying to help Ukraine become a democracy. Rather, Russia's incursion into a foreign country is the result of President Vladimir Putin trying to reclaim a lost Russian territory. Massie is Scotland editor for the Spectator *magazine.*

As you read, consider the following questions:

1. In what two other areas of Russia does Massie say the West made allowances for Putin's military actions?

2. What three other Western-allied countries does Massie suggest Russia could attack again?

3. With what other recent Western military invasion does Massie say Russia's occupation of Crimea should not be compared?

An astonishing number of useless twits appear to think Russia's annexation of the Crimea is somehow not Vladimir Putin's fault. The poor Russia despot—no longer much too strong a term, by the way—is not responsible for his actions. He was provoked!

Not simply by the Ukrainians, who should, it is implied, have known better, but by the West. It's our fault and Putin is simply acting logically and rationally. He has every right to reassert Russia's ancient prerogatives and if we hadn't penned him into a corner he wouldn't have needed to at all.

Twaddle of course but the kind of stuff that's not hard to find. Plenty of people—by no means confined to those you would not expect to know better—appear to be swallowing this nonsense. This is not a matter of right or left since you can find MPs from all quarters prepared to give Putin's absurd "referendum" some credence. Meanwhile, the anti-EU monomaniacs are happy to blame the crisis on Brussels and quietly—or not so quietly in fact—are thrilled to see *someone* tell the EU where to shove its (supposed) expansionary dreams. If that means cheering on Putin, then so be it. Any ally in a storm.

Another theory asks us to believe Putin's invasion and annexation of the Crimea was forced upon him by the West's expansion into Russia's sphere of influence. We should never have offered Ukraine any kind of guarantee. We should not have extended Kiev any kind of friendly hand. We certainly should not have allowed former members of the Warsaw Pact the opportunity to join NATO. By doing so we provoked Russia. What else would we expect? It's all our fault.

Of course Russia has no security concern in the Crimea. It was not threatened, nor were the rights or safety of ethnic Russians on the peninsula. Russia's access to its military bases in the Crimea was confirmed by treaty. Russia was not threatened by encirclement or anything of the sort.

But even if it were, that would still not remotely justify Russia's actions. The Crimea, as I've suggested before, is not the prize. The prize is Ukraine itself. Putin has made it quite clear he does not consider Ukraine a proper country. It is really part of Russia. Always has been. Always will be. A possession that got away, not an independent state in its own right.

So far Putin has not won Ukraine. Indeed it seems likely that he is awakening a renewed sense of Ukrainian patriotism. Including, in many instances, amongst Russian-speaking Ukrainians who have shown precious little interest in being reunited with Mother Russia. By "reunited", of course, I mean, "imprisoned".

Putin's actions in Russia should have been enough to warn the West that dealings with Moscow be conducted through gritted teeth. A man whose allies were (almost certainly) happy to bomb his own capital just to smooth his route to power is not, and never was, a man to be trusted or granted the benefit of the doubt.

In fact the international community has been extremely generous to Putin. We "understood" his concerns in the Caucasus and turned a blind eye to his war crimes in Chechnya. That really was a strange and foreign land in a faraway place about which we knew little and cared less. But we understood Russia's determination to protect its own territorial integrity. Besides, we couldn't really stop him even if we had wanted to. Not that Chechnya was worth anything to us. So we have spent many years *understanding* Russia's position.

But Ukraine is not Chechnya. It is part of Europe. So much so, in fact, that for a long time a large part of Ukraine was ruled from Vienna. Each day that passes is another day in

Russia Is at Fault in Ukraine Conflict

In most conflicts, there is a middle ground, but not when it comes to the Ukraine conflict. This entire mess in the south and east of Ukraine was completely orchestrated by Vladimir Putin who used the revolution as a pretense to justify his actions. . . .

This tragic crisis was begun after Putin's corrupt Ukrainian ally Viktor Yanukovych fled the country when deep public resentment was displayed. . . . Yanukovych dodged a much-discussed EU [European Union] trade agreement that won him the presidency, in favor of closer ties with Russia and the CIS [Commonwealth of Independent States]. The Russian deal also came with a 15 billion dollar loan for the cash-strapped Ukrainian government, but the people had had enough. In retaliation for losing Ukraine in the Russian-dominated CIS, Putin seized control of Crimea after a bogus referendum in which 97 percent of the population allegedly voted. . . .

Russia is currently gearing up for another incursion within the east of Ukraine after the Minsk peace agreement that has never been honored by the pro-Russian separatists that Putin is actively arming. Ukraine has responded to these obvious preparations for an offensive by sending reinforcements to key positions like Mariupol. Putin again used the reflective reasoning to say that Ukraine's forces are the ones preparing for an offensive, contrary to facts. Many photos and satellite data show Russian equipment entering the east of the country. It has to be the worst kept secret in the world that Russia is in the Ukraine, and yet Putin constantly denies this.

Justin Hillstead, "Russia Is the Only Country at Fault in the Ukraine Conflict," Euromaidan Press, November 27, 2014.

which Putin is denied his prize but it is also the case that a feeble Western reaction to Russia's aggression might be worse than no response at all. Deploying a miniature stick is worse than deploying no stick at all and, instead, keeping it in reserve for future use.

Dismembering and destroying Ukraine is Russia's goal. Anything short of that constitutes defeat for Moscow. Denying Putin that prize must now be the West's mission. If that means taking a financial hit, so be it.

Otherwise what use are our security guarantees? Putin, remember, is acting off the cuff here. This is not some masterly piece of deep and cunning Russian strategy. On the contrary, it is a piece of improvisation. That means Putin's momentum can be stalled and his advance on Kiev thwarted.

But only by stiffer, sterner action than we have seen heretofore.

Indeed, Putin's behaviour demonstrates that, if anything, the problem with NATO expansion is that perhaps it did not go far enough. What price the independence of Estonia, Latvia and Lithuania if they were not now members of the Western alliance? Even now their liberty is not guaranteed. It is not hard to see how Russian agitators could spark a contrived crisis in the Baltic states; not hard either to see how Putin might attack them again.

But NATO and the EU offer the Balts some protection. Thankfully. They have endured enough—as has the Ukraine, of course—at Russian hands in the past.

Nor, since we're on the subject, is Putin's behaviour George W. Bush's fault. The invasion of Iraq was, obviously, controversial. It neither set a precedent for nor justified Russia's recent behaviour. In the first place, everyone—even Russia—agreed that Iraq was in material breach of UN Security Council resolutions; secondly the US and its allies were hardly in the business of annexing Iraq for themselves.

But even if they had been and even if Bush's war set a rotten precedent, that would not justify Putin's actions either. Unless you do think one wrong must be matched with or by another. So, no, this isn't Bush's fault. It's not Tony Blair's fault either.

A few weeks ago, the idea that Ukraine might join NATO would have seemed fanciful. It no longer does. The West has a choice now: abandon Ukraine or not. And if we do will our treaty obligations to the Baltic states mean anything or will we abandon them too?

A test, then, of Western resolve but also, of our word and even, if you like, some kind of honour. Time may not be on Putin's side, but Western cravenness can still allow Putin to salvage something from his reckless blundering.

In other words, talking about the need to "de-escalate" matters might do more damage than escalating them and making it clear that Russia's actions will have consequences.

We—that is, the West—are not responsible for Putin's behaviour. But we are responsible for our response to his provocations.

"It's called peacemaking, not peacekeeping. There is no other country better positioned to do it than Russia."

The Russian Military Should Fully Invade Ukraine

Brad Cabana

In the following viewpoint, Brad Cabana argues that Russia should invade Ukraine to stop the civil war that is raging there. Only Russia possesses the authority to do this, Cabana claims, as it is supporting the Ukrainian rebels who are fighting the Ukrainian army. After the Russian army creates peace in Ukraine, Cabana contends, an international vote could be held on whether Ukraine's rebelling regions should remain with Ukraine or join Russia. Cabana is a blogger at the Rock Solid Politics *blog and a retired captain in the Canadian Armed Forces.*

As you read, consider the following questions:

1. What problem does Cabana say is making the war in Ukraine a war of attrition?

2. What kind of declaration does Cabana say Russia should make in the Ukrainian republics of Donetsk and Luhansk?

3. What does Cabana say is Russia's responsibility as a member of the international community?

It's a big leap for a writer in the West to advocate Russian military action in the Ukrainian republics of Donetsk and Luhansk. A stretch for sure. But, there is a sound case for it.

Russian Salvation

First is the nature of the warfare being conducted in the two republics. It started as a low-level, small unit–type internal insurrection. However, after the Ukraine army was unable to take Slavyansk with this type of action, it switched to larger and larger caliber weapons—including aircraft and helicopter gunships. To make a long story short, the Ukraine army drove the separatist forces almost to the Russian border before they were defeated and forced to retreat to the approximate lines that they occupy today.

The problem with the Ukraine war is that it is essentially World War II–type warfare without the air power. That essentially makes it like World War I warfare. A battle of attrition. Massive artillery replacing air power. Massive destruction and civilian casualties. Long bloody battles for meters that often get overturned by pointless counterattacks. No decisive battles or maneuvering. Just one layer of defence after another eating men and machines. A gristly affair that has no end other than internal political revolt or foreign intervention. It's the latter I suggest is necessary.

Someone has to intervene militarily in this conflict to tear apart the two sides who have a bloodlust for each other. Pure hatred that cannot be cured, and that must be dealt with by equally deadly force. Given that the conflict is happening on the border with Russia it is only logical that Russia should be the force to intervene.

One approach would be for Russia to declare a "hostilities free zone" in the republics of Donetsk and Luhansk. To back that declaration, Russia should position a large enough force to be militarily convincing on its border. Then, as a second step, Russia should impose air superiority over the area, engaging any artillery, from either side, that violates the hostilities free zone. Then, as the third step, Russia should move its ground forces into the two republics. Ukraine military units would be required to vacate the two republics. If they refused, they would be engaged and neutralized. Separatist forces would be required to marshal their men and equipment at certain points within the republics. If they refused, a similar fate would await them as Ukrainian units that failed to comply.

Once the forces are separated, and order is restored, the international community would hold a referendum in the two republics to determine if they wish to remain in Ukraine or become their own country, or a part of Russia, or any combination thereof.

Russian, Not Western, Responsibility

It's called peacemaking, not peacekeeping. There is no other country better positioned to do it than Russia. There is no country with a greater interest, other than Ukraine itself, in the restoration of peace and order in Donetsk and Luhansk. Additionally, as a responsible member of the international community, it is Russia's responsibility to bring an end to the war crimes being conducted by both sides, although more so by Ukraine forces, in Donetsk and Luhansk. Russia doesn't need anyone's permission to do this. Fact is, if it tried to get that permission it wouldn't be granted, and the bloody conflict will continue to consume tens of thousands of lives. It's realpolitik for a real situation. The West should butt out, and in effect mind its own business. The current situation comes as a direct result of the West interfering in Ukraine affairs to begin with. If you believe that the overthrow of the previous Ukraine president was just a spontaneous combustion of patriotic fervor, well, I have a bridge I'd like to sell you. Simply isn't true.

It's time to stop the insanity in Ukraine by peacemaking. The geopolitics means the cleanup job is Russia's responsibility. Hopefully, that will mean less civilians, especially the children, will die in a modern-day . . . war in Ukraine.

"Ethnically, historically and politically, Crimea does not belong to Ukraine."

Crimea Belongs to Russia

Dmitry Tamoikin

In the following viewpoint, Dmitry Tamoikin argues that Russia is correct in taking Crimea from Ukraine because the region has long been culturally Russian. Aside from this, Tamoikin contends, the Crimean and Ukrainian people dislike one another, and Ukraine should have given its territory of Crimea the democratic right to determine its own future. It is understandable, Tamoikin concludes, that Crimea should have wanted to rejoin Russia. Tamoikin is the chief executive officer of Earth Sphere Development Corporation.

As you read, consider the following questions:

1. Into what three ethnic groups does Tamoikin divide the population of Crimea?

2. What benefits does Tamoikin say Crimea will gain from its association with Russia rather than Ukraine?

Dmitry Tamoikin, "Crimea Belongs to Russia, Ukraine Does Not: What West Needs to Understand About Crimea," Shoutoutuk.org, January 3, 2014. © 2014 Shout Out UK. All rights reserved. Reproduced with permission.

3. What ethnic Crimean minority does Tamoikin say opposes Crimea's reunification with Russia?

I support the Ukrainian people in their fight against corruption and their desire for self-determination, regardless if
that means closer ties with the West or the East. That said,
ethnically, historically and politically, Crimea does not belong
to Ukraine. It is predominantly populated by Russians and
pro-Russian Ukrainians. Historically it has been Russian territory since the 18th century. Lastly, the political views of the
Crimean people are well represented by the Russian flags that
are now nearly on every government building in Crimea.
Overwhelmingly Crimean people speak, read, write and prefer
the Russian language over Ukrainian. Most important of all, if
given a democratic choice to stay with Ukraine or reunite
with Russia, Crimean people would overwhelmingly vote to
reunite with Russia.

What are my reasons for writing this [viewpoint]? I feel
the need to speak out because I see a clear absence of English-
language content from the Western media that is for Crimean
reunification with Russia. Even less is heard from the people
that truly have the right to talk on this subject; primarily
those who lived and still live in Crimea. My hope is to lead by
example and start a productive discussion on this important
matter.

My qualifications to talk on this subject are simple. I'm
both a Canadian citizen since 1996 and a Russian citizen by
birth and blood. Furthermore, my grandmother is Ukrainian
which makes me ¼ Ukrainian as well. However, what really
gives me the right to speak is the fact that I was born in Sevastopol, Crimea. I lived there for a long time and have a desire
to live there again. To date, I have two places that I can hon-
estly call home, they are: Halifax, Nova Scotia, and Sevastopol,
Crimea. Finally I have great respect for Ukrainian people and
have many friends as well as business partners who you may
call 100% Ukrainians. It is a wonderful country that is unfor-

tunately going through not so wonderful times. Please keep that in mind as you read what I have to say. . . .

Truly Autonomous

Ethnically Crimea is nearly 60% Russian, 20% Ukrainian, who are mainly pro-Russian, and roughly 14% Tatars. Other minorities are there as well and mostly support Russian reunification. Because historically Crimea has been Russian, and under modern Ukraine pro-Russian, most Ukrainians that do not like Russia have either moved out of Crimea or do not move there to live, in the first place. That is the reality of the situation. Only the Tatars who consider Crimea as their historic land, do not, on mass scale, support reunification with Russia. Their reasons I will discuss later in detail.

Politically, Crimean people are stuck with Ukraine but are looking high and low for ways out. Under the Ukrainian "management", Crimea has suffered extensively, while similar by climate Russian regions, like Sochi, have not just prospered extensively but held 2014 Olympic Winter Games. That tells something. Under the Ukrainian rule, the people of Crimea felt isolated and racially discriminated against, and forgotten by the central Kiev government; clashes between Russian and Tatar populations have only escalated, while the government has done almost nothing to prevent them; the unique ecosystem and natural beauty of Crimea has been neglected and irreversibly damaged, pollution is widespread and is a big problem; finally extensive poverty and criminal activity have flourished in Crimea making it the worst criminal region in Ukraine. Due to these and many other pressing reasons, the Crimean people no longer have confidence in the Ukrainian government.

Many Westerners may get the idea that Crimea is a state like any other in Ukraine, and it now wishes to go rogue, thus breaking the country apart. That is not the case. What most people call Crimea is technically called the Autonomous Republic of Crimea and it is unlike any other region in Ukraine. First of all, it has its own constitution, which currently accepts the Ukrainian law, but can be amended not to, by a referendum. Second, the title "Autonomous Republic" is there for a reason as well. Basically it means that Crimea is allowed a wide range of self-governance while willfully remaining part of the Ukraine. At a certain point, Crimea even had its own president; however, later he was removed and many self-governing aspects of Crimea were taken away by Kiev. The willful aspect is dissipating rapidly and all that Crimea has to do is hold a referendum to leave Ukraine. Now that is a very realistic scenario. This by the way is not a new idea to the West, nor should it be frowned upon. For example, many Canadians know that Quebec, a predominantly French-speaking province, twice has held a legitimate referendum, first in 1980 and second in 1995, to separate from Canada. It lost both times in a fair, open and democratic way. Crimea is no different in its right to hold such a referendum. Win or lose then will be solely up to the people. Now that is exactly what is taking place where people of Crimea want the same option to vote on whether to remain with Ukraine or reunite with Russia. In a democratic society, to which Ukraine is clearly striving, that choice must be given, if not to every province or state, then surely to provinces, states or republics that have autonomous status. The only thing that needs to be added is that under current conditions in Ukraine, Crimea is no longer asking, it is telling.

Ukrainians and Crimeans

What about the Ukrainian people in the rest of the country? Don't they have the right to decide their future, how to live their lives, what language to speak and with whom to ally? Don't they get to vote on the Crimean issue? To be blunt—no they don't. They would if Crimea was not an Autonomous Republic, but it is and that allows it to be a country within a country. By the way, an almost identical right was in fact given to Quebec after its two attempts to separate. Needless to say, the majority of Crimean people are not Ukrainian. They are predominantly Russian and they also have the right to choose their future, how to live their lives, what language to speak and with whom to ally.

Some point out that Crimea is not connected to Russia while it is connected to Ukraine. To that there is a very simple answer: Just like Alaska to United States, or Kaliningrad to Russia, Crimea has no problem with being disconnected from Russia by land while reuniting with it. It is as simple as that and it has been done before by other developed nations. . . .

Ukraine must allow Crimea, who is after all autonomous, just like Canada allowed Quebec, to decide its own future by democratic referendum. That is what democratic countries do.

There is no doubt, should Crimea join the Russian Federation, almost all of its people will be better off. That is a fact. They will be better paid, have lower crime rates, have better social securities, have better medical care, have much stronger economy and overall much more happy people. In turn, there is no doubt that under Ukrainian rule, Crimea is guaranteed to experience the full downturn of the Ukrainian economy, segregation and forceful integration of its predominantly Russian population (which will resist) and of course little protection against evermore radical Muslim Tatars. The fact of the matter is this, behind closed doors Ukrainian leaders do not care about Crimea; they see it as enemy state and will always put other Ukrainian regions first. Personally I think they have every right to do so, because the above said is true in reverse; Crimean people do not much care for Ukraine and will always put Crimean interests first. This dislike of one another is exactly why Crimea needs to separate. This is especially true of all new Kiev leaders that are now coming to power. In fact

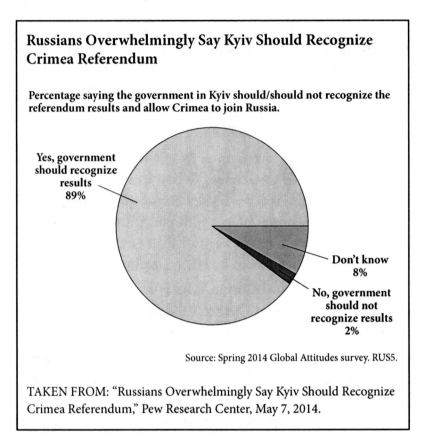

Russians Overwhelmingly Say Kyiv Should Recognize Crimea Referendum

Percentage saying the government in Kyiv should/should not recognize the referendum results and allow Crimea to join Russia.

Yes, government should recognize results 89%

Don't know 8%

No, government should not recognize results 2%

Source: Spring 2014 Global Attitudes survey. RUS5.

TAKEN FROM: "Russians Overwhelmingly Say Kyiv Should Recognize Crimea Referendum," Pew Research Center, May 7, 2014.

now more than ever, they are set against the Russians, since they not only don't support them but are a real threat to new administration. . . .

Right to Self-Determine

In light of all this talk about division, I wish to be absolutely clear. To me it is unthinkable that two brotherly nations would take up arms against each other over political disputes that have questionable origins. That must be avoided at all cost, even if that means Crimea is to remain with Ukraine.

The only minority that is against Crimean reunification with Russia are the Muslim Tatars. The reason for that is clear. The Tatars ultimately wish to have Crimea as their own autonomous Muslim state, similar to Chechnya in Russia, but preferably not even as part of Ukraine or any other nation. Under the much stronger Russian government, Tatars feel that the chances of such a state are impossible to achieve while under any Ukrainian government, especially a pro-European one, their chances are very high. That is their primary reason for resisting any reunification with Russia. Other reasons include religion. The age-old conflict of Muslims vs. Christians is still very much a reality in Crimea. There are historic reasons as well. Tatars and the Ottoman Empire were defeated by the Russians on multiple occasions, eventually losing Crimea completely in the 18th century. That history created a lot of bitterness in the Tatars and a great desire to regain supremacy in the region someday. Something that they have been in fact doing successfully so far, even under [Viktor] Yanukovych's rule! . . .

All Westerners that think that Crimean people should remain with Ukraine should ask themselves if they personally would want to live under the rule of any past or current Ukrainian government. Would they relocate from their nation to live and work in Ukraine right now or in the near future? I certainly would not and I think, predominantly, the answer of most Canadians, Americans or Europeans would be the same. At the same time, many Westerners live and work in Russia, which is not perfect but is very profitable to many top international businessmen. If that is the case, which it is, no one other than the Crimean people has the right to decide under which rule they should live. And one is clearly better for them than the other. If Crimean people suddenly decided that they should be part of Canada, that is their right, the question would arise, if Canada will accept a new province to its territory. The answer to this silly question is no. Interestingly enough, the only other country that would take Crimea and all of its people, problems and debt is Russia. If Crimea, on its own separates from Ukraine, Russia would unquestionably accept it as part of its territory. Why? The answer is clear. It was

Russian territory until 1954, the majority of the population there is Russian and would gladly accept Russian passports, and finally the people of the Russian Federation would welcome this long-awaited reunion as well.

The Best Future

With all above said, it is easy to analyze and debate although much harder to give a clear call for action and then stand behind it, for better or worse. At the risk of ridicule from my pro-Western colleagues, I shall do just that. My proposition to Crimea, to Ukraine, to Russia and to the West is as follows: Russia suspends its attempts to force Ukraine back into the preexisting geopolitical alliance and allows Ukraine on its own to determine its future, even if it includes closer ties with the West. In turn, Ukraine must allow Crimean people the freedom to vote if they wish to be part of Russia, Ukraine or form their own nation.

I have no doubt that if such an option was presented, Crimea would join the Russian Federation. Ironically, it is highly unlikely that Crimean people would have done so without the Kiev uprising, and yet following the example of Euromaidan [a movement that began in November of 2013 with public protests demanding reforms that were caused by the disruption of Ukraine's European integration] they are doing just that. Kiev protesters truly have given a historic opportunity to the Crimean people that otherwise they may never have had.

> *"There was no 'referendum' in Crimea.*
> *This 'referendum' was a cover for overt*
> *military aggression against Ukraine."*

Crimea Belongs to Ukraine

Yulia Tymoshenko

In the following viewpoint, Yulia Tymoshenko argues that Crimea belongs to Ukraine, since the Russian-controlled referendum in which Crimea rejoined Russia was illegitimate. Russia duped the Crimean people into joining it, Tymoshenko writes, promising them a powerful economic haven when in fact none exists. Ukraine, Tymoshenko believes, is a bastion of democracy that the Ukrainian people will not allow Russia to overthrow. Tymoshenko is the former prime minister of Ukraine and the leader of the All-Ukrainian Union "Fatherland" political party.

As you read, consider the following questions:

1. What document does Tymoshenko say will allow Ukraine to appeal to the International Criminal Court concerning the Russian annexation of Crimea?

Yulia Tymoshenko, "Yulia Tymoshenko: Crimea Will Always Be Ukrainian," CSMonitor .com, March 20, 2014. © 2014 Christian Science Monitor. All rights reserved. Reproduced with permission.

2. What myth about Russia does Tymoshenko say the Russian government has destroyed by its actions in Ukraine?

3. What does Tymoshenko say was Ukraine's first victory in its battle for European values?

First and foremost, on March 16 [2014] there was no "referendum" in Crimea. This "referendum" was a cover for overt military aggression against Ukraine and an attempt to annex part of Ukrainian territory.

Not a single civilized state has recognized the results of this so-called "referendum." It was 100 percent illegal, and its legal consequences are worthless. This big lie won't last long.

Justice over Crimea

Second, Crimea will always be Ukrainian, despite all the attempts of Russian occupants. This is our land and we won't give it away to anyone!

Third, from the bottom of my heart, I want to thank everyone who is defending Ukraine's national interests in Crimea in these dramatic days. I am grateful to Ukraine's military for their unbreakable spirit, forbearance, incredible heroism, and patriotism. I am grateful to the Crimeans who didn't support the separatists. I am grateful to the Crimean Tatars, the volunteers, and the journalists.

Thanks to you, a new proud and beautiful Ukraine is being born—a country of heroes! And there's nothing the Russian aggressors can do about this. Justice will be restored soon.

I implore the Ukrainian parliament to urgently ratify the Rome Statute to allow Ukraine to appeal to the International Criminal Court in The Hague and to petition the Constitutional Court of Ukraine to rule on the compatibility of the Rome Statute with the constitution of Ukraine. Ukraine must urgently appeal to the International Criminal Court to stop the military capture of Ukraine. Everyone involved in the military aggression against our state must face personal international responsibility.

Distorted Realities

I feel sorry for the people of Crimea who fell for this big lie and became victims of their own carelessness and naïveté, which may cast their sunny island into darkness. The Russian regime will soon show them that even the subtropics can have polar nights. This could lead to a humanitarian disaster and unpredictable consequences for the Crimeans. There will be no economic paradise. Russia doesn't have the resources— their economy is on the verge of collapse. Now that leading countries of the world are imposing the strictest sanctions against Russia, tomorrow they will have no interest in Crimea and its people.

Fourth, I feel sorry for the people of Russia. They are being led into a totalitarian abyss of economic and spiritual collapse, which goes hand in hand with poverty and devastation.

Using degrading and immoral means, the Russian government has destroyed the notion of truth with their mad propaganda for the occupation of Ukraine. They have killed the myth of Russia's orthodoxy, spirituality, and sacredness and what they believe is their positive personal role in the history of mankind. Instead, the whole world has witnessed Russia's immoral and unjustified aggression that has put under question the peaceful coexistence of all nations on this planet.

The Russian regime has even offset Russia's historical role in World War II and transformed it from a liberator to an invader. This moral loss for Russia is far more tragic than any perspective material losses resulting from international sanctions.

But we can only hope that a new Russia is also being born today. Not [Russian president Vladimir] Putin's Russia, but a country that last weekend [in March 2014] came out for the

Crimea Is Still Ukraine

One year ago, the Ukrainian territory of Crimea was illegally annexed by our neighbor and partner at the time, the Russian Federation. One year ago, as Russian special forces sacked the regional parliament and silenced dissenting voices, a farce referendum was held to position Moscow's land grab behind a facade of legitimacy. . . .

The annexation of the Ukrainian peninsula was not only an assault on international law, it also robbed Ukrainian citizens the right to live in their own state. Moscow quickly exported its strong-arm rule, cracking down on dissent, the media and access to information. Those who refuse to accept Russian citizenship are considered foreigners, given no protections against deportation and denied access to basic services. . . .

On March 27, 2014, 100 United Nations member states voted in favor of a resolution affirming support for the territorial integrity of Ukraine and recognition of Crimea as a part of Ukraine. We remember and appreciate this display of international solidarity in a time of need. And we believe that the Crimean people will regain their native land.

One year later, Crimea still is Ukraine, and it is our joint responsibility with the rest of the world to undo the injustice de facto and de jure—to make the aggressor go. Sooner or later Crimea will return to where it belongs, and our joint duty is to make it sooner—out of respect of the rights of our citizens, to international law and for the sake of safeguarding global security.

Petro Poroshenko, "Crimea Is Still Ukraine,"
Wall Street Journal, *March 19, 2015.*

march of freedom. A Russia of Andrey Makarevich [Russian rock musician] wearing a yellow and blue ribbon. A Russia of Liya Akhedzhakova [Russian actress], Eldar Ryazanov [Russian film director], and Boris Grebenshchikov [Russian rock musician]. Ukraine has a real future with a Russia like this.

A Strong Ukraine

Fifth, on the Maidan [square], Ukraine made its pro-European choice and gained its first victory in the battle for European values by removing the dictatorship. Today, despite all the difficulties, our unity is stronger than ever before. On March 21 we will see the signing of the Association Agreement with the European Union. This is a success for Ukraine and it cannot be erased. Let nobody doubt our resilience and assuredness.

We made our choice and we choose freedom! . . .

We are a peaceful people who do not choose war. But if necessary, we can do more than just defend ourselves. Perhaps even against our will, Ukraine now has a new and greater mission: to help break the tyranny of our neighboring state with our spiritual and moral power.

Ukraine has learned to win and today has the strongest weapon in the world—the power of will, honor, truth, and spirit!

Today Ukraine is not only the geographical center of Europe; it is also the spiritual center for the victory of democracy. The world has recognized this and is standing by Ukraine's side.

Last Saturday, Valeriya Novodvorskaya [a Russian dissident] said democratic Russia is waiting for the Ukrainian army to liberate it. This is obviously a metaphor, but it does contain a grain of reality.

We won't be visiting anyone with tanks and machine guns, but we have a different army. It is an army that cannot be stopped by borders, trenches, anti-tank fortifications or minefields. It is our Ukrainian army of freedom, democracy, human dignity, and spirit. And it is already on the march. Ukraine is fulfilling its mission, which includes the liberation of Russia.

I believe that everything will be fine.

(P.S. According to legend, Master Kano [referring to Kano Jigoro] was walking through the forest in winter and saw two tree branches covered in snow. One thick branch broke under the weight of the snow whilst another, a younger branch, bent under the weight, straightened back up, throwing the snow. This is how judo came to be—a martial art whose basic principle is to feign submission in order to win. But only feign. Ukraine is that second, younger branch. I think there's at least one well-known judoka in Russia that should know this parable [referring to Vladimir Putin, who has practiced judo since he was a young boy].)

Periodical and Internet Sources Bibliography

The following articles have been selected to supplement the diverse views presented in this chapter.

David A. Andelman "Keep Putin Talking to Save Ukraine," *USA Today*, February 17, 2015.

Timothy Garton Ash "There'll Be No Peace While Putin Is Squatting in Ukraine's Living Room," *Guardian*, February 16, 2015.

Doug Bandow "Ukraine's War with Russia Isn't America's Fight," *Japan Times*, May 15, 2015.

Theunis Bates "Ukraine's Fraught Relationship with Russia: A Brief History," *The Week*, March 8, 2014.

Alexander Golts "Is the Ukraine Conflict a Victory or Defeat for Russia?," *Moscow Times*, April 27, 2015.

Gustav Gressel "The Ukraine-Russia War," European Council on Foreign Relations, January 26, 2015.

Katharine Lackey and Oren Dorell "Ukraine-Russia Conflict: What You Need to Know," *USA Today*, August 31, 2014.

James Rubin "Putin Won't Stop on His Warpath Until Timid NATO Shows It Has Teeth," *Sunday Times* (London), February 1, 2015.

Timothy Snyder "Ukrainian Extremists Will Only Triumph if Russia Invades," *New Republic*, April 17, 2014.

Tom Switzer "Huff and Bluff: Putin's Crimea Incursion Just a Case of Russia Protecting Home Turf," *Sydney Morning Herald*, June 3, 2014.

William Taylor, Steven K. Pifer, and John E. Herbst "Don't Forget Crimea," *New York Times*, June 8, 2014.

OPPOSING
VIEWPOINTS®
SERIES

CHAPTER 4

How Should Ukraine Plan Its Future?

Chapter Preface

Ukraine's war in its Donbass region began soon after Russia annexed Ukraine's Crimean peninsula in March of 2014. The event, in which the Russian military oversaw the Crimean parliament's vote to secede from Ukraine and become a federal subject of Russia, inspired other pro-Russian separatists in southeastern Ukraine, an area known as the Donbass, also to call for independence from Ukraine. These separatists then declared the Ukrainian oblasts, or administrative divisions, of Donetsk and Luhansk independent states. The Ukrainian government refused to let these regions secede from Ukraine, and fighting subsequently erupted between the Ukrainian military and the rebels.

In April of 2014, weeks after the fighting began, Russian president Vladimir Putin referred to Ukraine's Donbass region as "Novorossiya," or New Russia. This was the name used in eighteenth- and nineteenth-century imperial Russia to denote the Ukrainian lands conquered by the Russian tsar. Putin listed Donetsk, Luhansk, Odessa, Kherson, Kharkiv, and Mykolaiv—all cities in either eastern or southern Ukraine—as areas formerly part of New Russia that the Soviet Union returned to Ukraine in the 1920s.

However, the Donbass's history of intertwined Ukrainian and Russian ownership began before the Soviet era. From the sixteenth to the eighteenth centuries, a state called Zaporizhian Sich, inhabited by the East Slavic Cossack people, existed in the western Donbass before being taken over by the Russian Empire. The state was a predecessor to the modern Ukraine, as its inhabitants spoke the Ukrainian language and participated in their own Ukrainian culture. Cossacks in the eastern Donbass retained control of their land until 1918, after the Soviet Union absorbed the entirety of Ukraine, albeit with its southern and eastern territories intact.

From the mid-eighteenth century to the present, throughout its numerous changes in political domination, the Donbass has remained an industrial, working-class area, sustained mostly by metallurgy and coal mines. However, it was the cultural and historical identity of the people of the Donbass that was called into question during the armed conflict that began there in 2014. Supporters of Ukraine claimed that all Ukrainians, from west to east, were united by one culture and history; Russian nationalists simultaneously believed that the Donbass was Russian in everything but name, as Russia had formerly occupied the region and only returned it to Ukraine to appease the country after its Soviet takeover.

Despite numerous cease-fire agreements negotiated between Ukraine and Russia in Minsk, Belarus, the conflict in Ukraine continued raging. In the midst of the war, the Donbass separatists declared the oblasts of Donetsk and Luhansk as autonomous people's republics, entities not recognized by the majority of the international community. As the rebels vowed to uphold the security of their self-proclaimed states, Ukrainian president Petro Poroshenko continued Ukraine's efforts to retake separatist-held lands.

The following chapter presents viewpoints relating to the political future of Ukraine, of which the eventual outcome of the war in the Donbass is a crucial component. Topics covered in this chapter include Ukraine joining the North Atlantic Treaty Organization (NATO); Ukraine's loans from the International Monetary Fund (IMF); whether fighting for control of the Donbass is worth Ukraine's effort; and which parties in the Ukrainian conflict are responsible for committing war crimes.

> *"The West either must do what it can to support Ukraine's military effort, or it may have to admit that international borders need to be redrawn."*

Ukraine Must Hold On to Its Contested Regions

William Risch

In the following viewpoint, William Risch contends that the West should help Ukraine hold on to the Donbass, the Ukrainian region being fought over by the Ukrainian military and Russian-supported Ukrainian rebels. Ukraine was guaranteed protection against foreign aggressors after gaining its independence, Risch writes, and the United States and Europe must now follow through on their promises. This ultimately must be done, he believes, so that Russia does not make mockeries out of international agreements. Risch is a contributing writer at the Ukraine Crisis Media Center in Kiev, Ukraine.

As you read, consider the following questions:

1. What military initiative does Risch say Ukrainian armed forces renewed after experiencing attacks by pro-Russian militants?

2. What document does Risch say had Ukraine exchange its Soviet nuclear stockpile for Western military protection?

3. Besides using military force, what else does Risch say Western countries can do to help Ukraine fight its war for the Donbass?

L ast night [July 1, 2014], Ukraine's president, Petro Poro-shenko, told his nation that they were at war. The Ukrainian government, after attempting peace talks for several days, was ending its unilateral cease-fire with pro-Russian forces in the Donbass region, which it has been fighting for over two months. "They have publicly declared their unwillingness to support the peace plan as a whole and particularly the cease-fire," he said. "Militants violated the truce for more than a hundred times." Thus Ukrainian forces, including the army, national guard, ministry of interior forces, and paramilitary battalions have officially renewed the anti-terrorist operation (ATO).

Gathering Forces

This time, the ATO promises to be an all-out war. Since the cease-fire took effect June 20, both Ukrainian and rebel forces have reinforced their positions. More tanks, rockets, personnel, and supplies from across the Russian border have reached pro-Russian forces. The Ukrainian online news source InfoResist reported June 30 that separatist Igor Girkin (aka Strelkov), after complaining for weeks about a lack of support from Russia, had assembled a force capable of seizing Izium, the headquarters of Ukraine's ATO: 5,000 armed men in Sloviansk and dozens of armored equipment, tanks, and multiple rocket launchers. Fresh reinforcements have arrived in nearby Krasnyi Lyman and Kramatorsk. InfoResist stressed that Strelkov not only could take Izium, but also advance toward major industrial city of Kharkiv, due to the Ministry of Internal Affairs forces lacking heavy armament.

Facing forces like Strelkov's, Ukraine's ATO will cost many lives. It will make worse a refugee crisis that has already led to at least 27,200 internally displaced persons from eastern Ukraine as of June 27, according to a recent United Nations High Commissioner for Refugees (UNHCR) report. The hundreds of military and civilians killed could reach the thousands if air strikes and artillery assaults become even deadlier.

Despite the nightmarish scenario, all-out war looks inevitable. There is not even one hint that the forces of the Donetsk People's Republic (DPR) or the Luhansk People's Republic (LPR) even took President Poroshenko's cease-fire seriously. During it, their forces killed a total of 27 Ukrainian security forces personnel and wounded 69. DPR and LPR leaders have suggested plans for creating a larger entity, New Russia (Novorossiya), which would incorporate other regions of eastern and southern Ukraine. On June 26, one of their key supporters—Oleh Tsarev, one of their representatives in peace talks with the Ukrainian government—announced competitions for designing national symbols for Novorossiya and a history textbook for the start of the new school year.

Territorial Integrity

In the face of war, neither the United States nor the European Union can afford to let Ukraine lose the Donbass [a region in eastern Ukraine]. The Budapest Memorandum [on Security Assurances] of 1994, which led to Ukraine giving up its stockpiles of Soviet nuclear weapons, guaranteed that the Russian Federation, the United Kingdom of Great Britain and Northern Ireland, and the United States of America would refrain

145

Budapest Memorandum on Security Assurances

The Budapest Memorandum on Security Assurances is a diplomatic memorandum that was signed in December 1994 by Ukraine, Russia, the United States, and the United Kingdom.

It is not a formal treaty, but rather a diplomatic document under which signatories made promises to each other as part of the denuclearization of former Soviet republics after the dissolution of the Soviet Union. . . .

In the Budapest Memorandum, Russia, the United Kingdom, and the United States promised that none of them would ever threaten or use force against the territorial integrity or political independence of Ukraine. They also pledged that none of them would ever use economic coercion to subordinate Ukraine to their own interest.

They specifically pledged they would refrain from making each other's territory the object of military occupation or engage in other uses of force in violation of international law.

All sides agreed that no such occupation or acquisition will be recognized as legal and that the signatories would "consult in the event a situation arises which raises a question concerning these commitments."

Ron Synovitz, "Explainer: The Budapest Memorandum and Its Relevance to Crimea," Radio Free Europe, Februray 28, 2014.

from using force "against the territorial integrity or political independence of Ukraine, and that none of their weapons will ever be used against Ukraine except in self-defence or otherwise in accordance with the charter of the United Nations." Over the past few weeks, Russia's lending separatists advanced weaponry and armed volunteers from across the border has seriously threatened Ukraine's territorial integrity. What looked like a local conflict lacking popular support at the beginning of June has turned into a full-scale invasion at the beginning of July. This invasion and Russia's illegal seizure of Crimea have made a total mockery of the Budapest memorandum.

Supporting Ukraine's war for the Donbass does not mean sacrificing the blood and treasure of U.S. or E.U. [European Union] member forces. Western countries could send military advisors to train a more effective army (one badly undermined by corruption over the past quarter century). They could send ammunition. They could help finance the construction of a more secure border between Russia and Ukraine. Most importantly, they could support more vigorous economic sanctions against Russia. The West either must do what it can to support Ukraine's military effort, or it may have to admit that international borders need to be redrawn and that international guarantees like the Budapest Memorandum are mere scraps of paper.

> *"Kiev's best way out of Putin's trap may be to withdraw from the Donbas territories controlled by Russian troops and separatists."*

Ukraine Should Give Up Its Contested Regions

Alexander J. Motyl

In the following viewpoint, Alexander J. Motyl argues that Ukraine should stop fighting the war with pro-Russian rebels in its Donbass (or Donbas) region. Doing so would help Ukraine escape from Russia's trap of burdening it with instability, violence, and economic drain. Without having to worry about the Donbass, Motyl claims, Ukraine could continue integrating itself with the West. Motyl is a professor of political science at Rutgers University.

As you read, consider the following questions:

1. According to Motyl, why did Russian president Vladimir Putin prefer to let secessionist movements grow in Ukraine's Donetsk and Luhansk regions rather than invade the areas himself?

2. What does Motyl say would be the strategic goal, as the situation relates to Russia, of Ukraine pulling out of the Donbass?

3. What does Motyl claim was Putin's ultimate goal for eastern Ukraine when Russian forces invaded it?

B y now, most observers of the ongoing conflict between Russia and Ukraine assume that Russian president Vladimir Putin aims to annex the Donbas region of Ukraine and, possibly, other parts of the country's southeast, which his regime has taken to calling "New Russia." But that leaves open two questions: First, why didn't Putin invade Ukraine immediately after he seized Crimea in early March [2014]; and second, why, if he intends to hold the Donbas, would he allow his proxies to shell cities, kill civilians, and destroy mines, plants, schools, and other infrastructure?

Russia's Show of Strength

In a recent interview with Marat Gelman, a political commentator for the liberal Russian publication *Novoye Vremya*, Vladimir Lukin, a veteran policy maker who served as Putin's human rights commissioner from February 2004 to March 2014 and who represented Russia in the West's negotiations with Ukrainian president Viktor Yanukovych and the democratic opposition on February 20, offered some answers.

According to Lukin, the Donbas isn't the goal at all: "No one in the Kremlin needs the Donetsk People's Republic, the Luhansk People's Republic [the self-styled secessionist entities in the Donbas], or New Russia," he said. Indeed, "to win the Donbas and to lose Ukraine would be a defeat for the Kremlin." When pressed further about the purpose of the Kremlin's agitation in the region, Lukin responded that one should "forget the Donetsk and Luhansk People's Republics. The goal is to demonstrate to [Ukrainian president Petro] Poroshenko that he cannot win." Russia, he said, would "introduce as many [troops] as necessary to persuade Poroshenko that he must negotiate with whomever Putin chooses." In his commentary about the interview, Gelman went on to explain that, according to Lukin, both Donetsk and Luhansk will serve "as guarantees of [Ukraine's] nonmembership in NATO [North Atlantic Treaty Organization]." After all, "any referendum on joining any bloc would have to take place in every region, and if only one were against, then the country could not join." The Kremlin's ideal outcome, according to Lukin, is that "everything should go back to as it was under Yanukovych, but without Yanukovych."

When asked how long the violence would continue, Lukin explained, "We're in no hurry. [Poroshenko] is the one who needs to hurry. Or else the girl with the braid"—former prime minister Yulia Tymoshenko—"will eat him up. Poroshenko's chair is on fire beneath his butt, not ours." But people do not need to continue to die. "It was because of the false certainty of the Ukrainians that they could win that they proceeded so actively with the anti-terrorist operation," Lukin explained. Now, "everyone sees they cannot win" and so "the most militarily active stage has passed."

Putin's Gamble

Lukin's statements make some sense. First, they provide an answer to the question of why Putin didn't seize the opportunity to invade Ukraine earlier in the conflict. The Ukrainian government and army were completely disorganized after the Maidan [square] revolution, and a quick strike could have won Putin Kiev. If Lukin is right, an invasion may never have been in the cards. Instead, Putin may have placed his hopes on the secessionist movements that formed the Donetsk and Luhansk People's Republics as a way to get him what he wanted at lower cost. When those failed to win a decisive victory and to prevent a Ukrainian rollback, Putin intervened. In the last few days, he seems to have halted and partially reversed the Ukrainian advance.

Second, Lukin's talking points explain the mass destruction. As a result of separatist rule and the ensuing war, several thousand civilians have been killed and wounded, and hundreds of thousands have fled their homes. In addition, industrial production in Donetsk province has fallen by 29 percent. In Luhansk, it has crashed by 56 percent. Taken together, both provinces have experienced a 46 percent decline in light industry, a 41 percent drop in the chemical industry, a 34 percent crash in machine building, a 22 percent fall in construction materials, a 19 percent decrease in pharmaceutical production, a 13 percent loss in metallurgy, and a 13 percent drop in the coal industry.

If the proxies' goal was to "liberate" the Donbas and its Russian residents, then why destroy the territory and make life impossible for the residents? But if, as Lukin suggests, the goal was to ensure that the Donbas remains within Ukraine to thwart integration with NATO and to provide Russia with leverage over Kiev, then maximal devastation would go a long way toward promoting Russia's political goals. A devastated region would be an economic drain on Kiev's scarce resources and a source of never-ending political instability. It would also invite continued Russian offers of humanitarian aid, particularly for the region's reconstruction, which would enable the Kremlin to continue influencing politics in Ukraine without having to try to swallow the whole country.

Seen in this light, defeating the pro-Russian rebels and the Russian regular forces (estimated to number between 5,000 and 15,000) could be impossible, and accommodating them would be counterproductive. Even if Ukraine liberated the region, as it promises, it will be saddled with a devastated, unstable, and permanently insecure rust belt that will continue to do what it has done since independence in 1991: serve as a

Russia Refuses to Take Donbass from Ukraine

President Vladimir Putin in February [2015] turned down an offer from his Ukrainian counterpart Petro Poroshenko to "take the Donbass"—the area in the country's east that is currently partly controlled by pro-Russian insurgents—and asked Poroshenko whether he was "out of his mind," *Forbes* magazine reported Monday [in April 2015].

Putin reportedly told a closed-door meeting with senior board members of the Russian Union of Industrialists and Entrepreneurs on March 19 that Poroshenko had offered him eastern Ukraine's Donbass region—which includes the war-torn Donetsk and Luhansk regions—at peace talks in Minsk at which a cease-fire was agreed in February, according to an unidentified source cited by *Forbes* who participated in the meeting.

According to the source, Putin recounted the overnight Minsk negotiations, saying: "[Poroshenko] told me directly: 'Take the Donbass.' I replied: 'Are you out of your mind? I don't need the Donbass. If you don't need it, declare it independent,'" *Forbes* reported. . . .

A spokesman for Ukraine's Foreign Affairs Ministry, Yevhen Perebyinis, blamed a linguistic misunderstanding for the report, apparently suggesting Poroshenko had spoken in Ukrainian and Putin had misunderstood him.

"Poroshenko did not tell Putin to 'take the Donbass' but told him to 'get out of it,'" Perebyinis said Monday on his Twitter account.

Ivan Nechepurenko, "Putin Refused Poroshenko's Offer to 'Take Donbass'—Forbes," Moscow Times, April 6, 2015.

channel for Russian influence on Ukraine's internal affairs and a home to political forces—whether among the separatists or among Yanukovych's formerly dominant Party of Regions— that oppose reform and integration with the West.

The Best Way Forward

If that is the case, then Kiev's best way out of Putin's trap may be to withdraw from the Donbas territories controlled by Russian troops and separatists. The goal would be to turn them not into autonomous federal units within a weak Ukraine, as Putin desires, but into an independent entity, as he pointedly does not. Having turned the tables on Putin, Kiev could then request Western assistance for enhancing its military's defensive capacities, including building fortifications along its new frontier with Russia and the rump Donbas. Russia and its proxies would then have to clean up the mess they made in the Donbas, Ukraine would be free to pursue integration with the West and the world, and the United States and Europe could breathe a little easier, knowing that the bloodshed had come to an end.

Of course, all this assumes that Lukin really does know Putin's mind and was honest in his exchange with Gelman. There is evidence to support both assumptions. On August 31, Putin called on Kiev to begin "substantive, content-filled negotiations about the . . . political organization of society and the state in southeastern Ukraine," suggesting that the goal of the recent Russian invasion of eastern Ukraine was to lure Kiev into agreeing to some form of federalization for the Donbas. But even if Lukin's account was inaccurate, Kiev would still have to realistically assess its chances of retaking those parts of the Donbas controlled by Russia—and of trying to rule those territories afterward. If it decides that its chances of success are small and declining, and that the territories would be impossible to manage, formally abandoning the Donbas and attempting to rebuild a Western country may permit Ukraine to snatch victory from the jaws of defeat. By the same token, saddling Putin with two economic sinkholes— Crimea and the Donbas—could only hasten his regime's decline.

Understandably, Ukrainians—and especially their ambitious political leaders and courageous volunteer battalions— will be unwilling to accept such a solution, arguing that soldiers' and civilians' lives weren't sacrificed for the satisfaction of Putin's imperial designs and that calls to withdraw from the Donbas enclave controlled by Russia are tantamount to treason. Morally, they will be right. And Putin, no doubt, is banking on such morally uncompromising views to influence Ukrainian policy as well. Considering the alternatives, however, Ukrainians might be wise to refuse to play the game on his terms and focus only on what is best for them and their country. If they come to believe that the choice is between constant war, a return to things as they were "under Yanukovych, but without Yanukovych," or genuine independence within manageable frontiers, they may decide that abandoning an ungovernable stretch that was always Ukraine's odd man out would actually be a stunning example of Ukraine's commitment to real sovereignty.

And who knows? When Putin eventually exits the political stage and Russia tires of Putinism's misdeeds, the Donbas and perhaps even Crimea may come knocking on Ukraine's door. If they do, Ukraine could readmit them on its own terms, not on the Kremlin's.

| *"Amnesty International calls on all parties, including Russia, to stop violations of the laws of war."*

Ukraine Must Prosecute Those Committing War Crimes

Amnesty International

In the following viewpoint, Amnesty International contends that the Ukrainian military and pro-Russia separatist forces are each responsible for committing war crimes in Ukraine's internal fighting. The author claims that both sides have subjected Ukrainian citizens to indiscriminate artillery shelling and have carried out kidnappings, torture, and murder. Amnesty International believes that Ukrainian authorities should investigate all those suspected of committing these crimes so that innocent Ukrainians are spared the side effects of the ongoing war. Amnesty International is a nongovernmental organization that advocates for human rights.

Amnesty International, "Ukraine: Mounting Evidence of War Crimes and Russian Involvement," Amnesty.org, September 7, 2014. © 2014 Amnesty International. All rights reserved. Reproduced with permission.

As you read, consider the following questions:

1. What does Amnesty International cite as new evidence that the war in Ukraine has burgeoned into an international armed conflict?

2. What does Amnesty International claim happened after residents of the city of Sloviansk collected the ransom for a pastor kidnapped by separatist forces?

3. What Luhansk militia group does Amnesty International claim has been committing war crimes in the Ukraine civil war?

Ukrainian militia and separatist forces are responsible for war crimes, Amnesty International said today [in September 2014]. The organisation accused Russia of fuelling separatist crimes as it revealed satellite images indicating a buildup of Russian armour and artillery in eastern Ukraine. Despite a fragile cease-fire, the situation on the ground remains fraught with danger and Amnesty International calls on all parties, including Russia, to stop violations of the laws of war.

"All sides in this conflict have shown disregard for civilian lives and are blatantly violating their international obligations," said Salil Shetty, Amnesty International's secretary general, who travels to Kyiv and Moscow in the coming days. "Our evidence shows that Russia is fuelling the conflict, both through direct interference and by supporting the separatists in the east. Russia must stop the steady flow of weapons and other support to an insurgent force heavily implicated in gross human rights violations."

International Armed Conflict

Amnesty International researchers on the ground in eastern Ukraine have documented incidents of indiscriminate shelling, abductions, torture, and killings. The Kremlin [referring to the Russian government] has repeatedly denied any involvement in the fighting in Ukraine, but satellite imagery and testimony gathered by the organization provide compelling evidence that the fighting has burgeoned into what Amnesty International now considers an international armed conflict. The images show new artillery positions being established just inside the Ukrainian border between 13 and 29 August, including what appear to be 122-mm howitzer D-30 artillery units in firing positions pointed toward the west. Two of the positions have a support vehicle and what looks like bunkers.

On 29 August, six armoured amphibious vehicles (likely BRDM-2s) can be seen. Another similar artillery position can be seen in a field northeast of the first, also within Ukrainian territory. Imagery from 26 August 2014 shows six relatively advanced self-propelled howitzers (likely 2S19 Msta-S 152-mm) in firing positions facing southwest at Ukrainian army locations. Between 26 and 29 August 2014 the artillery has been moved into a west-facing firing position still within Ukraine. On August 29 the imagery shows what look like numerous military vehicles in the area along the tree line and in the neighboring field. "These satellite images, coupled with reports of Russian troops captured inside Ukraine and eyewitness accounts of Russian troops and military vehicles rolling across the border, leave no doubt that this is now an international armed conflict," said Shetty.

Civilians and War Crimes

Amnesty International researchers on the ground in eastern Ukraine interviewed eyewitnesses fleeing from fighting near Alchevsk, Donetsk, Kramatorsk, Krasnyi Luch, Lisichansk, Luhansk, Rubizhne, Pervomaisk and Sloviansk. Researchers also interviewed Ukrainian refugees in the Rostov region of Russia. Civilians from these areas told Amnesty International that the Ukrainian government forces subjected their neighbourhoods to heavy shelling. Their testimonies suggest that the attacks were indiscriminate and may amount to war crimes.

Witnesses also said that separatist fighters abducted, tortured, and killed their neighbours. In an illustrative incident, residents of Sloviansk told Amnesty International that separatist fighters kidnapped a local pastor, two of his sons and two churchgoers, and requested a US$50,000 ransom for their release. By the time the local community managed to collect the requested ransom, the witnesses said, the captors had killed all of the men.

Amnesty International has also received credible reports of abductions and beatings carried out by volunteer battalions operating alongside regular Ukrainian armed forces. For example, on 23 August a security guard in Oleksandrivka, Luhansk region was seized by several dozen armed men who arrived in vehicles flying Ukrainian flags. At least one was marked "Battalion Aidar" (a militia group operating in the Luhansk region). Witnesses said his captors accused him of collaborating with separatists, beat him with rifle butts and held him incommunicado until 27 August, when his family was informed he was being held in another town, in the local office of Ukraine's state security service.

Amnesty International is calling on the Ukrainian authorities to conduct an effective investigation into allegations of serious violations of international humanitarian law and bring to justice individuals responsible for war crimes. Commanders and civilian leaders may also be prosecuted for war crimes as a matter of command responsibility if they knew or should have known about the crimes and failed to prevent them or punish those responsible. "Civilians in Ukraine deserve protection and justice," Salil Shetty said. "Without a thorough and independent investigation, there's a real risk Ukrainians will harbour the scars of this war for generations."

"The coup regime in Kiev is throwing its most aggressive and abusive . . . battalions under the bus to preserve its image."

Ukrainian Military as a Whole Is Responsible for War Crimes

David Garrett

In the following viewpoint, David Garrett argues that little international attention is being paid to the Ukrainian military's human rights abuses in Ukraine's armed conflict. Just as pro-Russia separatist forces are indiscriminately killing civilians, he contends, so, too, are members of the Ukrainian army and the volunteers fighting alongside them. Garrett believes that this shows a mainstream media bias against Russia in support of the new Ukrainian government. Garrett is a contributor to the Centre for Research on Globalization website.

As you read, consider the following questions:

1. What major criminal offense does Garrett say Amnesty International has accused separatists, but not Ukrainians, of perpetrating?

2. What does Garrett say has now happened to the Yatsenyuk junta that seized power in Kiev?

3. What qualities of Ukraine's MiG-29 and Su-27 combat aircraft does Garrett believe make it likely that Ukraine shot down Malaysia's Flight MH17 passenger jet?

On 05 September [2014], Amnesty International, a nongovernmental organisation [NGO] focused on human rights, published "Ukraine: Mounting Evidence of War Crimes and Russian Involvement."

Clear Bias

Analysis of the 738-word Amnesty article reveals clear bias in the NGO's reporting on the conflict in eastern Ukraine. Amnesty makes more than twice the effort to place blame for human rights abuses and possible war crimes on separatist forces and "Russian troops" (380 words) than on Ukrainian government forces (140 words).

Amnesty explicitly accuses separatists of "torture," a major criminal offense under international law. Amnesty makes no mention of "torture" in association with the regular Ukrainian armed forces or those designated 'bad apples,' the Aidar Battalion [a volunteer military unit of the Armed Forces of Ukraine].

Salil Shetty, Amnesty International's secretary general, states unequivocally:

> "Our evidence shows that Russia is fuelling the conflict, both through direct interference and by supporting the separatists in the east. Russia must stop the steady flow of weapons and other support to an insurgent force heavily implicated in gross human rights violations."

The evidence presented to support these accusations is a "series of satellite images commissioned by Amnesty International." The images appear to have been provided by a non-profit organization called the American Association for the Advancement of Science [AAAS]. According to its website, AAAS analyzes high-resolution satellite images collected by "publicly accessible commercial satellites." In other words, the images come from the United States.

Shetty delivers the punchline:

> "The Kremlin has repeatedly denied any involvement in the fighting in Ukraine, but satellite imagery and testimony gathered by the organization provide compelling evidence that the fighting has burgeoned into what Amnesty International now considers an international armed conflict."

Predictably, Amnesty has declared what complicit NATO [North Atlantic Treaty Organization] officials and compliant mainstream media have long been insisting, without the benefit of evidence: Russia has 'invaded' Ukraine.

Pure Capability

On 07 September, Amnesty published a briefing on "Abuses and War Crimes by the Aidar Volunteer Battalion in the North Luhansk Region." The briefing contained carefully worded language that depicts the Ukrainian government forces as lawful actors, the 'good guys' in the conflict:

> "The Ukrainian authorities cannot afford to replicate in the areas they retake, the lawlessness and abuses that have prevailed in separatist-held areas. The failure to eliminate abuses and possible war crimes by volunteer battalions risks significantly aggravating tensions in the east of the country and undermining the proclaimed intentions of the new Ukrainian authorities to strengthen and uphold the rule of law more broadly."

The coup regime in Kiev is throwing its most aggressive and abusive Nazi volunteer battalions under the bus to preserve its image. The very forces that enabled the Yatsenyuk junta [to] seize and hold power in Kiev in February are being

Malaysia Airlines Flight MH17

One year ago [in July 2014], 298 people lost their lives when a Malaysia Airlines passenger jet crashed in eastern Ukraine, close to the border with Russia.

Flight MH17, en route from Amsterdam to Kuala Lumpur, was travelling over the conflict-hit region on 17 July 2014 when it disappeared from radar. A total of 283 passengers, including 80 children, and 15 crew members were on board. . . .

Western nations believe there is growing evidence that the plane was hit by a Russian-supplied missile fired by rebels. However, Russia blames Ukrainian government forces.

US officials from the Office of the Director of National Intelligence have said there is a "solid case" that a SA-11 missile . . . was fired from eastern Ukraine under "conditions the Russians helped create".

They say the "most plausible explanation" for the shooting down of the plane was that rebels mistook it for another aircraft.

Evidence includes images purportedly showing a surface-to-air missile launcher in the area, analysis of voice recordings of pro-Russian rebels apparently admitting bringing the airliner down and social media activity pointing to rebel involvement.

Russia, however, denies all allegations it supplied weaponry to the rebels and has instead suggested a Ukrainian military plane flew within firing range of the airliner just before it came down. The Ukrainian government rejects the claims.

BBC News, "MH17 Malaysia Plane Crash: What We Know," August 11, 2015.

sacrificed as the requisite 'few bad apples,' thereby freeing the mainstream media to focus all its attention on the 'real' baddies: "Russian troops" that support "an insurgent force heavily implicated in gross human rights violations" in eastern Ukraine, according to Amnesty.

On 08 September, Amnesty published an article declaring that "Ukraine Must Stop Ongoing Abuses and War Crimes by Pro-Ukrainian Volunteer Forces." Amnesty's statements appear to be part of a dedicated effort to insulate the regular Ukrainian armed forces from accusations of abuses and possible war crimes, which may include Ukrainian Air Force responsibility for the 17 July downing of Malaysia Airlines Flight MH17.

Ukrainian Air Force MiG-29 "Fulcrum" and Su-27 "Flanker" jet fighter aircraft have dominated the skies over eastern Ukraine since the early days of Kiev's 'anti-terrorist operation.' The separatist forces have no aircraft and no functioning surface-to-air missile systems capable of striking aircraft above 11,000 feet. No Russian Federation combat aircraft have flown over eastern Ukraine.

MiG-29 and Su-27 both have service ceilings near 60,000 feet and are easily capable of high-speed combat maneuvers at MH17's reported cruising altitude of 33,000 feet. Both jet aircraft are armed with the GSh-301 single-barreled, recoil operated 30mm cannon, which alone is capable of causing explosive decompression in a commercial passenger airliner. In combination with a laser range-finding/targeting system, the GSh-301 is a powerful and extremely accurate weapon, capable of destroying a target with as few as three to five rounds. The gun's maximum effective range against aerial targets is 200 to 800 m.

Ukrainian combat aircraft losses in eastern Ukraine include one MiG-29 shot down near the village of Zhdanivka, 40 kilometres northeast of Donetsk, on 7 August 2014; and one MiG-29 shot down near Luhansk on 17 August 2014. No Su-27 combat losses have been reported so far.

"Stability hinges on the West agreeing not to pull Ukraine into NATO or the EU."

Why Ukraine Shouldn't Be Offered NATO Membership

Andrei Tsygankov

In the following viewpoint, Andrei Tsygankov contends that Ukraine should not be allowed to join the North Atlantic Treaty Organization (NATO), for this could provoke Russia into further military violence. Russia already views Western meddling in Eastern European politics as dangerous, Tsygankov writes, and the NATO army on Russia's border with Ukraine would cross an unacceptable line. Instead, he believes, Ukraine should retain its status quo and continue enjoying relative stability from its appeased Russian neighbor. Tsygankov is a contributing writer for the Frontliner news site.

As you read, consider the following questions:

1. What two countries does Tsygankov say blocked Ukraine from joining NATO in 2008?

2. What does Tsygankov cite as examples of Russia's various dangerous incidents with NATO planes since March of 2014?

3. What two factors does Tsygankov say have made Russians view Western nations as Russia's enemies?

There are plenty of reasons why the West wants to rein Russia in. The war with Georgia in August 2008, the recent annexation of Crimea and the hybrid war in Ukraine are all evidence of expansionist behaviour that concerns Europe and the United States. Some see arming Ukraine, and making it a NATO [North Atlantic Treaty Organization] member, as the best way of achieving stability. This, however, is a dangerous idea.

Russian Escalation

There are reasons to believe that the move will provoke Russia, a country that already feels threatened by the West's growing influence in Eastern Europe ever since the collapse of communism.

To Russian foreign policy experts NATO remains one of the most tangible threats to the country. That is no surprise, given that it was created as a Western alliance against the Soviet Union.

In 2008, the United States first started openly pushing for Georgia and Ukraine's membership in the alliance. At the time, Russia responded with alarm. As early as June 2006, Russia's foreign minister said that Ukraine or Georgia joining NATO could lead to a colossal shift in global geopolitics. Fearful of the consequences of admitting the countries into the alliance, France and Germany managed to block membership at the NATO summit in April 2008, which was held in Bucharest.

It is not just NATO that has Russia on edge. The United States and other leading Western nations like France, Britain

Russia Objects to Ukraine as a Member of NATO

Russia said on Wednesday [December 24, 2014] NATO [North Atlantic Treaty Organization] was turning Ukraine into a "front line of confrontation" and threatened to sever remaining ties with the Atlantic military alliance if Ukraine's hopes of joining it were realized. . . .

It is likely to take years for Ukraine to meet the technical criteria for accession to NATO and, even then, there is no certainty that the alliance is ready to take such a political hot potato.

Yet Russia has made clear it would see the NATO membership of such a strategic former Soviet republic with a long common border as a direct military threat.

Thomas Grove, "Russia: If Ukraine Joins NATO, We 'Will Respond Appropriately,'" Business Insider, December 24, 2014.

and Germany, endorsed the "color revolutions" in former Soviet countries like Georgia, Kyrgyzstan and Ukraine, which were seen as highly destabilizing by Russia.

Then, in February 2014, Western governments supported the Maidan [square] protests in Kiev, which the Kremlin [Russian government] feared could be a prelude to revolution in Russia itself. As President Vladimir Putin put it in his Crimea speech, "with Ukraine, our Western partners have crossed the line, playing the bear and acting irresponsibly and unprofessionally."

The tense standoff that followed between the West and Russia resulted in an ever-worsening situation in Ukraine and the widest-ranging sanctions against Russia since the end of the Cold War [referring to nonviolent political and military tension between the United States and the Soviet Union, beginning after World War II and lasting until 1991]. Relations keep hitting new lows, and will only deteriorate further if NATO membership for Ukraine remains on the Western agenda.

Is the West prepared for an aggressive response by Putin to the perceived NATO threat?

Russia and Western Resolve

Putin has boldly tested the West's will on numerous occasions. The European Leadership Network recently issued a report in which it documented about 40 dangerous incidents between Russia and NATO planes since March 2014. The incidents included "violations of national airspace, emergency scrambles, narrowly avoided midair collisions, close encounters at sea, simulated attack runs and other dangerous happenings," according to the report.

Among the routine skirmishes taking place, there have been 11 "serious" incidents, such as Russian planes flying unusually close to Western warships. More worryingly still, three incidents last year ran a high risk of leading to either casualties or direct military intervention. The 'submarine hunt' in Swedish waters in October, the Russian abduction of a veteran Estonian intelligence officer in September, and a near-collision of a Russian surveillance plane with an SAS [Scandinavian Airlines] flight from Copenhagen, Denmark, to Rome in March: All of these incidents could have led to unintended escalation.

Meanwhile, the West seems unwilling to respond to Russia with resolve. Russia seized the Estonian officer a mere two days after President Barack Obama visited Tallinn [the capital of Estonia] and promised Estonia full military support. NATO and the European Union [EU] called for a strong response to

the incident, but so far no such response followed, indicating the lack of will to engage with an aggressive Russia.

In Russia, support for robust actions only grows stronger by the day. Due to the economic sanctions and domestic propaganda campaign, the overwhelming majority of Russians now view the Western nations as enemies seeking to destroy Russia and its leaders. If need be, the Kremlin will have no serious difficulty finding public support for an outright military intervention in Ukraine.

Future Stability

The solution to this is not NATO membership for Ukraine. Such a move will only contribute to turning Russia from an angry but manageable power into a real enemy and, possibly, starting a wider war in Europe.

Stability hinges on the West agreeing not to pull Ukraine into NATO or the EU. For the time being, it is beneficial to have Russia as a co-provider of Ukraine's security and development, together with the West.

In a longer run, a new conference on European security must be called to formally end the post–Cold War era and establish a security system with Russia and Ukraine as key players.

> "IMF money doesn't go to the country
> and it doesn't go to the people. It goes
> to the billionaires who run them."

Taking IMF Money Would Damage Ukraine's Economy

*Jeffrey Sommers and Michael Hudson, as told
to Jessica Desvarieux*

*In the following viewpoint, Jeffrey Sommers and Michael Hud-
son, as interviewed by Jessica Desvarieux, argue that the International Monetary Fund's (IMF's) large loans to Ukraine will
only hurt the country's poor and working-class people. They
claim that this is because the money will either be immediately
used to pay off Russian debts or be taken by the billionaires who
run the country. Rather, Sommers and Hudson suggest, Ukraine
needs to work to build up its own local economies to create jobs.
Sommers is a senior fellow at the Institute of World Affairs at
the University of Wisconsin–Milwaukee. Hudson is a professor of
economics at the University of Missouri–Kansas City. Desvarieux
is a journalist for the Real News Network.*

Jessica Desvarieux, "Who in Ukraine Will Benefit from an IMF Bailout?," TheRealNews
.com, October 3, 2014. © 2014 TheRealNews.com. All rights reserved. Reproduced with
permission.

As you read, consider the following questions:

1. According to Hudson, how much does Ukraine still owe Russia from the Soviet Union era, and for what?

2. What public domain entities does Hudson say Westerners will want to buy in Ukraine after the government privatizes them to pay its IMF loans?

3. What group of nations does Sommers say economists should study for effective development models that can help struggling Eastern European economies?

JESSICA DESVARIEUX, TRNN PRODUCER: Welcome to the Real News Network. I'm Jessica Desvarieux in Baltimore.

While much of the reporting on Ukraine has focused on the political battles between the U.S., the E.U. [European Union], and Russia, there's little coverage on the economic consequences of such battles for the debt-ridden nation, especially what this means for ordinary Ukrainians. The interim government in Ukraine is currently negotiating a $15 billion IMF [International Monetary Fund] bailout package, with talks set to conclude on March 21 [2015].

Also since the referendum and annexation of Crimea by Russia, the U.S. and E.U. have imposed sanctions on several Russian and Ukrainian politicians. That means visa bans and asset freezes for the elite. And there could be more coming down the pipeline, according to U.S. vice president Joe Biden.

Joining us now to discuss the economic aspect of the situation in Ukraine are our two guests.

Jeffrey Sommers is an associate professor and senior fellow of the Institute of World Affairs at the University of Wisconsin–Milwaukee [UWM].

Also joining us is Michael Hudson. He is a distinguished research professor of economics at the University of Missouri–Kansas City [UMKC].

Thank you both for joining us.

A Bad Deal?

So I'm going to first start off with you, Jeffrey. My first question is related to the conditions for a possible IMF deal. They include cuts to gas subsidies, pensions, public sector employment, as well as privatization of government assets, a deal that really sounds like it's going to hurt ordinary Ukrainians. So my first question is: What actually is behind them potentially accepting a deal like this? And why would they risk losing their political power?

JEFFREY SOMMERS, INSTITUTE OF WORLD AFFAIRS, UWM: Well, you know, I don't think they're going to risk losing their political power. Now, you're absolutely right. This is going to be terribly painful for the people of Ukraine. But what they're going to be able to do is just to deflect and to put the blame on the Russians for this and somehow suggest that this is all necessary and that there is a light at the end of the tunnel. So just as with the, frankly, Soviet rulers in the past, in terms of how they always promised a golden age off in the distance, Ukraine's rulers will do the same, and this will be echoed by remarks coming from the IMF.

Now, I would also say that they're also going to be pointing to Poland and the Baltic states. And they are going to say that, look, these are two places that went through the same kinds of conditions that we're going to be imposing upon you, and you are going to come out like them. Now, for people in Ukraine, Poland in particular will appear to be quite appealing, because the per capita purchasing power of people in Poland is literally twice that of Ukraine. . . .

DESVARIEUX: Alright. Michael, I want to ask you who aims to benefit from this IMF deal.

MICHEAL HUDSON, PROF. ECONOMICS, UMKC: Well, there are a number of—all of the money that has been given by the IMF and the West in the past has been given to the kleptocrats [rulers who gain at the expense of citizens] that run Ukraine. The UN [United Nations] and the World Bank have Ukraine right next to Nigeria for the GINI coefficient of concentrated income. So, basically, the Europeans have told the kleptocrats, the ten or 12 billionaires that run the country, we will make you very, very rich if you join us. We will give you a lot of IMF money, you can transfer it into your banks and your bank accounts, you can then send it abroad to your offshore banking centers, and the Ukrainian people will owe it. So you can do the Ukraine what the Irish government did to the Irish: You can take the public money, you can give it all to the private bankers, and then you can tax your people and make them pay.

But as soon as the IMF gives the loan to the Ukraine . . . Russia says that Ukraine owes $20 billion, dating back to the Soviet Union era in exchange for, in addition, to about $5 billion or $6 billion for the oil subsidies that it's been given. Russia said it is going to charge Ukraine the normal oil price, not the subsidized price. So all the money that the IMF and the U.S. give [to Ukraine,] Russia says is immediately owed to it itself.

Whatever happens, either the Russian government will get the IMF money for gas and imports or the kleptocrats will. None of the money—and I think Jeff agrees—none of this money's going to go to the Ukrainian economy any more than the IMF money went to the Irish economy or the Greek economy or the other economies that are there. IMF money doesn't go to the country and it doesn't go to the people. It goes to the billionaires who run them to take the money and immediately send it back to the West so it's a circular flow, and it goes in and out of Ukraine in about 20 minutes.

The Suffering Populace

DESVARIEUX: Michael, I'm glad that you brought up those countries as examples, 'cause I think it's important for us to get some historical context about the role of the IMF in the post-Soviet nations of Eastern Europe. You both have written

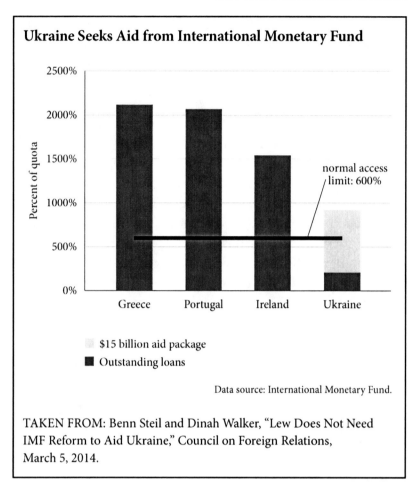

Ukraine Seeks Aid from International Monetary Fund

normal access limit: 600%

$15 billion aid package
Outstanding loans

Data source: International Monetary Fund.

TAKEN FROM: Benn Steil and Dinah Walker, "Lew Does Not Need IMF Reform to Aid Ukraine," Council on Foreign Relations, March 5, 2014.

about the IMF bailouts in Latvia. So, Michael, I'm going to ask you first: Can you talk about the consequences for the economy, particularly the working-class people, whether they're likely to see the same in Ukraine happen to them?

HUDSON: The objective of IMF loans is to deindustrialize the economy. It is to force the economy—meaning *the government* when you say *the economy*—the government has to pay the IMF loan by privatizing whatever remains in the public domain. The Westerners want to buy the Ukrainian farmland. They want to buy the public utilities. They want to buy the roads. They want to buy the ports. And all of this is going to be sold at a very low price to the Westerners, and the price that the Westerners pay will be turned over to the Ukrainian government, that then will turn it back to the Ukraine. So whatever the West gives Ukraine will immediately be taken back.

But not only will the money be taken back, but the Ukrainian factories, roads, infrastructure, bridges, farmland, and property will also pass into foreign ownership, just like it did in Russia, just like it did in Latvia, just like it does in all of the other post-Soviet countries. And then this is going to lead to lower wage payments. Many Ukrainians say they haven't been paid for two months. In Russia in 1994, during the [Russian president Boris] Yeltsin sell-off, labor went ten or 12 months without being paid. You can't pay labor and at the same time pay the IMF and pay the kleptocrats. Something has to give, and what gives is going to be living standards and labor.

So the result will be what it was in Latvia, Greece, and Ireland, where 20 percent of the population emigrated. Just like 20 years ago you had an influx of Polish plumbers into London, you're now going to have millions of Ukrainian plumbers pouring into Western Europe, saying, we want jobs at anything; there are no jobs at home.

Suffocating Industry

DESVARIEUX: Jeff, you're actually in Latvia right now. Can you speak to some of what Michael raised, those issues?

SOMMERS: Well, I'm not in Latvia at present, although I spend quite a bit of time there.

But much of what Michael says is correct. And just as I indicated, what the differences were with Poland and the kind of deal that Ukraine is going to get, we also have to remember that a country like Latvia will also be presented as an example of what the Ukrainians can aspire to. And we have to remember that they're just entirely different economies. So even if one took the position that Latvia has somehow been success-

Ukraine Is a Kleptocracy

With all the media frenzy centering upon hostilities in Ukraine, it's easy to lose track of the original goals of the Maidan [square] revolution which occurred one year ago. Just what was the revolt all about in the first place? It's a somewhat tricky question to ask since rebellion against the unpopular government of Viktor Yanukovych unfolded in distinct phases with constituencies often pushing conflicting agendas. . . .

Ukraine is reportedly the most corrupt country in Europe, even more so than Russia. Such realities have prompted the likes of Devin Ackles to sit up and take notice. Ackles, who works as an analyst for CASE Ukraine, a not-for-profit specializing in economic research, has remarked that "Ukraine has become one of the biggest kleptocracies in the world." . . .

"Shortly after independence in 1991," he writes, "a new tradition developed in Ukraine. People entered the government, whether at the local or national level, primarily to find ways to improve their financial standing by milking the system. When MPs [members of parliament] turn up to work in Range Rovers while sporting fancy tailor-made suits and unfathomably expensive timepieces, no one is fooled for a second that they were able to pay for these luxuries on their meager state salaries."

Ackles adds that many Ukrainians grew disillusioned with the 2004–5 Orange Revolution [a series of protests and political events that took place in Ukraine from November 2004 to January 2005], and people began to realize the country was dealing not just with a "few bad apples" but rather "the whole barrel was rotten."

Nikolas Kozloff "Welcome to Ukraine: One of the 'Biggest Kleptocracies in the World,'" Huffington Post, February 15, 2015.

ful, even though its people have just suffered massively over the past few years under the conditions of austerity, with huge numbers of people exiting, some 10 percent of the population since 2000, and, as Michael says, some, you know, almost 20 percent since independence in 1991, you know, these are very different economies that are based largely on offshore banking. They're very small. They can fulfill this kind of niche role that a big country like Ukraine just absolutely can't.

I mean, Ukraine's future is in grain production. And, as Michael says, you're going to see foreign companies coming in, hoping to assert control over that prime grain-producing land.

Now, also as Michael says, there's going to be a continuation of an already existing trend with Ukraine, and that is to, again, emigration. Now, the problem with this idea that somehow by joining the E.U. everything is going to be good for the people of Ukraine is that what Ukrainians are essentially seeing are the echoes of a social democratic past which is being euthanized in the European Union. So this whole idea of a social market, of a social Europe is one which they still can experience when they go abroad, but what they don't really understand is that structurally it's being destroyed. And so this is not the future, unfortunately, that they're going to inhabit if they join the E.U. It's more likely, again, to be just one of, unfortunately, some misery, especially for the working and the middle classes, as the subsidies for gas and for education and for the other necessities for reproducing a middle-class standard of living are taken away.

Now, to get to the issue of maybe what should be done, of course, what we need is an entire reassessment of the development model that we've seen in both the former Warsaw Pact [a treaty that included the Soviet Union, Albania, Poland, Romania, Hungary, East Germany, Czechoslovakia, and Bulgaria] nations and the former constituent parts of the Soviet Union. We need to look more at local production and at creating and satisfying more of their demands internally, you know, rather than thinking that just by being integrated into the European Union, that somehow there's going to be a market for their goods. There's not. The experience that we've seen in the past is that when these fragile economies get opened up even more so to those of West Europe, that their domestic industry really gets suffocated, and the only thing that they get in return are cheap consumer products. So I don't see much good coming out of this deal with the European Union or the IMF. . . .

DESVARIEUX: Alright, Jeffrey Sommers and Michael Hudson. Thank you both for joining us.

Periodical and Internet Sources Bibliography

The following articles have been selected to supplement the diverse views presented in this chapter.

Nick Butler   "Ukraine's Uncertain Future," *The Globalist*, January 2, 2015.

Susannah Cullinane   "Ukraine to Ask Hague to Investigate 'Crimes Against Humanity,'" CNN, January 26, 2015.

Economist   "Ukraine Before the Election: The Battle for Ukraine's Future," October 25, 2014.

Andrew Foxall   "To See Ukraine's Future, Recall Crimea," *New York Times*, March 24, 2015.

Peter Leonard   "Ukraine Rebels Killed Captive Soldiers, Claims Amnesty International," *Huffington Post*, April 9, 2015.

Peter Pomerantsev   "Is There a Future for Ukraine?," *Atlantic*, July 8, 2014.

Petro Poroshenko   "Ukraine's Future Is in Europe—We Have Chosen Our Path," *Guardian*, April 24, 2015.

Armine Sahakyan   "Ukraine Is Worst Victim of Russia's Export of Human Rights Abuses," *Kyiv Post*, May 15, 2015.

George Soros   "The New Russia, the New Ukraine, and Europe's Future," European Council on Foreign Relations, February 3, 2015.

Vessela Tcherneva   "Ukraine's Reform Crossroads," European Council on Foreign Relations, April 29, 2015.

Andrei Tsygankov   "Why Ukraine Shouldn't Be Offered NATO Membership," Reuters, January 12, 2015.

For Further Discussion

Chapter 1

1. Chris Freind argues that the United States should not intervene militarily in the Ukraine conflict, for an American war against Russia would expend too much effort to achieve an outcome that does not affect the United States at all. Is Freind correct in saying that the United States should ignore world conflicts that do not directly affect it? Explain.

2. Josh Cohen writes that the United States should not provide weapons to Ukraine because Russia would respond by further escalating the conflict, possibly by arming Iran. Does Cohen make a good point in claiming that the United States should avoid helping an ally simply because of the repercussions that may result? Should a country help its partners no matter the cost, or do friendly international relations have limits? Explain your reasoning.

3. David J. Kramer argues that the United States can stop Russian violence against Ukraine by implementing strict economic sanctions against Russia. Kramer says that doing so may lead European countries to impose their own sanctions against Russia. Do you think economic sanctions would deter Russian aggression? Explain your reasoning. If sanctions won't be effective, what do you think should be done to curtail Russian aggression in the region? Explain.

Chapter 2

1. After reading the viewpoints in chapter 2, do you think the United States and its allies should intervene in Ukraine? Additionally, do you think attempts to foment democracy around the world should be considered reck-

less meddling, or does the United States have a duty to do this wherever it can? Explain your reasoning.

2. Alexander Donetsky argues that Europe should not integrate Ukraine into the European Union. Doing this, he writes, would lead to an extended initial period of economic hardship for both the European Union and Ukraine, as the effects of Ukraine's collapsed economy would be felt by all Europeans. Should Europe exclude Ukraine from the European Union due to its temporary financial situation, or should it bear the cost of repairing Ukraine's economy now so it can become strong and successful later?

3. Seumas Milne believes that the expanded role of the North Atlantic Treaty Organization (NATO) in world affairs is what prompted Russia to invade and annex Crimea, for the Western military alliance was originally created as a defense against the power of the Soviet Union. Do you agree with Milne that NATO should curtail its efforts to ensure peace and security around the world so it does not risk antagonizing a belligerent Russia? Or are reactions like Russia's necessary by-products of such endeavors? Explain your reasoning.

Chapter 3

1. Alex Massie advocates for the United States enduring financial hardship, if necessary, to prevent Russia from invading and reclaiming the entirety of Ukraine for itself. Should maintaining the integrity of Ukraine's sovereignty warrant the United States risking any degree of economic security, or would the financial burden be worth the peace and stability that would eventually result in Ukraine and Russia? Explain your reasoning.

2. Brad Cabana believes that the Russian military should invade Ukraine to enact a truce between the Ukrainian military and pro-Russian rebels. Do you agree with Ca-

bana that Russia is the only military force with authority to do this, since Ukraine's war is taking place along the Russian border? Or is Russia too close to this conflict to mitigate it effectively? Explain.

3. Dmitry Tamoikin writes that it is only natural for Crimea to want to secede from Ukraine and join Russia, for most of the Crimean people are ethnically, historically, and culturally Russian. Do you think Tamoikin's argument is sound? Should the common ethnicity and culture of a group of people unequivocally permit them to self-determine their own national affiliations? Or does the international rule of law outweigh a people's desires for such ends? Explain.

Chapter 4

1. William Risch argues that neither the United States nor Western Europe should allow Ukraine to lose its Donbass region to separatists, since doing so would demonstrate to the world that the West could not follow through on its documented commitments to defend its allies. Should the West assist Ukraine in the Donbass only to be seen honoring its vows of protection, or should the West intervene there for strictly strategic purposes? Explain.

2. Alexander J. Motyl suggests that Ukraine give up its contested Donbass region to the Russian-backed separatists so it can avoid the economic and political hardships that would accompany reincorporating the area into the main Ukrainian government. Would following Motyl's advice be a practical decision for Ukraine? Does the pragmatism of Ukraine giving up the Donbass to its enemies trump the risk of appearing weak on the international stage? Explain your reasoning.

3. Andrei Tsygankov argues that Ukraine should not be allowed to join NATO because this could provoke Russia into further military violence against the country. Taking

into account that Russia cites NATO expansion as one of the reasons it invaded Ukraine, do you think Ukraine's membership in NATO would make the country safer from Russian aggression or more susceptible to it? Explain.

Organizations to Contact

The editors have compiled the following list of organizations concerned with the issues debated in this book. The descriptions are derived from materials provided by the organizations. All have publications or information available for interested readers. The list was compiled on the date of publication of the present volume; the information provided here may change. Be aware that many organizations take several weeks or longer to respond to inquiries, so allow as much time as possible.

American Center for a European Ukraine
Washington, DC
e-mail: info@europeanukraine.org
website: www.europeanukraine.org

The American Center for a European Ukraine is a public affairs institution devoted to covering news and generating commentary and recommendations on Ukraine's current political status and its journey toward full integration with Western Europe. The center is staffed by Americans and Europeans who have all acquired firsthand knowledge of Ukraine's current political, economic, and cultural situation so they can make informed suggestions on Ukraine's future. Articles on the Ukraine crisis and ongoing Ukrainian political developments can be accessed on the organization's website. The center's *Bulletin* provides in-depth commentary and reporting, with articles such as "Ukraine-Russia-West: Love Hate Relationship," "Is Russia Winning in Ukraine?," and "For Ukraine, It Is 'Reform or Die.'"

**American Enterprise Institute for Public
Policy Research (AEI)**
1150 Seventeenth Street NW, Washington, DC   20036
(202) 862-5800 • fax: (202) 862-7177
website: www.aei.org

Since its founding in 1943, the American Enterprise Institute for Public Policy Research (AEI) has worked to promote public policy that is in accordance with conservative ideals such as limited government, a strong national defense, and free market economics. In addition to crafting policy recommendations for the United States, AEI has researched and published extensively on the Ukraine crisis, calling for a peaceful Western response to Russian president Vladimir Putin's actions in Ukraine's civil war. The *American* is the monthly magazine of the AEI; articles from this publication and additional commentary and policy analysis are available on the organization's website.

Brookings Institution

1775 Massachusetts Avenue NW, Washington, DC   20036
(202) 797-6000
e-mail: communications@brookings.edu
website: www.brookings.edu

Based in Washington, DC, the Brookings Institution seeks to provide accurate, independent research to construct policy recommendations that will make the American democracy stronger, guarantee that all Americans have social and economic security and opportunity, and ensure that the international system remains stable and open. Essays examining the Ukraine crisis, including predictions and examinations of the future between Ukraine and Russia, can be accessed on the Brookings website. Opinion articles on Ukraine can also be found on the Brookings Institution's blog, *Up Front*.

Carnegie Endowment for International Peace

1779 Massachusetts Avenue NW
Washington, DC   20036-2103
(202) 483-7600 • fax: (202) 483-1840
e-mail: info@CarnegieEndowment.org
website: www.carnegieendowment.org

The Carnegie Endowment for International Peace works to achieve increased cooperation between nations and encourages the United States to take an active role in the international community. Amid the Ukraine crisis, the organization supported Ukraine's integration into Western Europe and the European Union, out of the sphere of Russian influence, as the Ukrainian civil war continued. *Foreign Policy* is the organization's bimonthly magazine; articles from this publication, additional reports, and commentaries are available online.

Cato Institute

1000 Massachusetts Avenue NW
Washington, DC   20001-5403
(202) 842-0200 • fax: (202) 842-3490
website: www.cato.org

The Cato Institute is a libertarian think tank advocating limited government involvement in social and economic matters and favoring a free market economy. Cato promotes a US foreign policy that provides sufficient protection for American sovereignty but does not cross the line into interventionism and empire building. Cato opposes American intervention in the Ukraine crisis, arguing that hostilities between Russia and Ukraine do not at all threaten US national security. The institute's main publication is the *Cato Journal*, which recommends public policy from a libertarian perspective. Copies of Cato studies, reports, and commentaries concerning Ukraine can be accessed on the institute's website.

Center for American Progress (CAP)

1333 H Street NW, 10th Floor, Washington, DC   20005
(202) 682-1611 • fax: (202) 682-1867
e-mail: progress@americanprogress.org
website: www.americanprogress.org

The Center for American Progress (CAP) seeks to promote a liberal and progressive agenda focused on ensuring that labor and civil rights are granted to all Americans. The organization believes that America should be an international leader to ensure peace and stability worldwide. CAP supports American intervention in Ukraine, calling for economic sanctions to punish Russia for its aggression in Ukraine and for long-term American aid to Ukraine itself. Reports and opinion articles on Ukraine can be found online at the CAP website.

Center for Strategic and International Studies (CSIS)
1616 Rhode Island Avenue NW, Washington, DC   20036
(202) 887-0200 • fax: (202) 775-3199
website: www.csis.org

Experts at the bipartisan Center for Strategic and International Studies (CSIS) research and analyze issues relating to defense and security policy, global problems, and regional studies to provide policy suggestions for individuals in government. The organization has supported a moderate US approach to the Ukraine crisis, advocating for American aid to Ukraine while attempting to de-escalate the country's war with Russian-backed rebels. Articles on the Ukraine crisis can be accessed online. The *Washington Quarterly* is the official publication of CSIS.

Council on Foreign Relations (CFR)
Harold Pratt House, 58 East Sixty-Eighth Street
New York, NY   10065
(212) 434-9400 • fax: (212) 434-9800
website: www.cfr.org

The Council on Foreign Relations (CFR) is a nonpartisan membership research organization that provides information on current foreign policy decisions and the process of foreign policy making. Educational materials are made available for both the public and policy makers in an attempt to foster informed debate and decision making. The organization has produced a wealth of policy studies on the Ukraine crisis, with many experts calling for American military aid for Ukraine to stave off further Russian aggression in the country. The bimonthly publication of CFR is *Foreign Affairs*; the CFR website offers copies of articles from this magazine as well as backgrounders, op-eds, and transcripts of testimony.

Heritage Foundation

214 Massachusetts Avenue NE, Washington, DC 20002-4999
(202) 546-4400 • fax: (202) 546-8328
e-mail: info@heritage.org
website: www.heritage.org

As a conservative public policy institute, the Heritage Foundation is dedicated to the promotion of policies consistent with the ideas of free enterprise, limited government, individual freedom, traditional American values, and a strong national defense. The Heritage Foundation has supported an active US role in the Ukraine crisis, advocating for diplomatic isolation of Russia and financial and military aid to Ukraine. Reports, commentaries, and articles on the Ukraine crisis, such as "Aid to Ukraine Should Not Be Held Hostage by IMF Politics," can be found on the Heritage Foundation's website. Also online is the foundation's Daily Signal platform, featuring articles such as "Why Ukraine Is a Mess and How It Got There" and "The Russia-Ukraine Conflict in Pictures, One Year After Crimea's Annexation."

Ukraine Crisis Media Center

Ukrainian House, European Square, 2 Khreshchatyk Street
Kyiv 01001
  Ukraine
+380 50 157 81 59
e-mail: press@uacrisis.org
website: http://uacrisis.org

The Ukraine Crisis Media Center was founded in March of 2014 as an international news outlet on the Ukraine crisis and the country's ongoing civil war with Russian-supported separatists. The center details events in Ukraine as they relate to national security, politics, the military, and human rights. Articles and videos on developments in Ukraine can be accessed on the organization's website.

United States Department of State
Harry S. Truman Building, 2201 C Street NW
Washington, DC 20001
website: www.state.gov

The US Department of State is the executive department charged with shaping and sustaining a peaceful, prosperous, just, and democratic world, as well as fostering conditions for stability and progress for the benefit of the American people and people worldwide. The State Department attaches great importance to the success of Ukraine's transition to a democratic state with a flourishing market economy. Its policy toward Ukraine is centered on strengthening a democratic, prosperous, and secure nation more closely integrated into Europe and Euro-Atlantic structures. The State Department website features a section on Ukraine that contains fact sheets, testimony, reports, and press releases. The State Department blog, *Dipnote*, features articles on Ukraine, including "One Year Later: Russia's Occupation of Crimea" and "Ukraine: Hope, Progress, and the Challenging Road Ahead."

Bibliography of Books

Anders Åslund   *Ukraine: What Went Wrong and How to Fix It.* Washington, DC: Peterson Institute for International Economics, 2015.

Paul Belker   *NATO: Response to the Crisis in Ukraine and Security Concerns in Central and Eastern Europe.* Seattle, WA: CreateSpace, 2014.

Janusz Bugajski, Steven Pifer, and Celeste Wallander   *Ukraine: A Net Assessment of 16 Years of Independence.* Washington, DC: Center for Strategic and International Studies, 2008.

William Dunkerley   *Ukraine in the Crosshairs.* New Britain, CT: Omnicom Press, 2014.

Hall Gardner   *NATO Expansion and US Strategy in Asia: Surmounting the Global Crisis.* New York: Palgrave Macmillan, 2013.

Brian Jenkins   *Crisis in Crimea: A Historical Lead Up to the Conflict Between Russia and Ukraine.* Seattle, WA: CreateSpace, 2014.

Henry Kissinger   *World Order.* New York: Penguin Press, 2014.

Andrey Kurkov   *Ukraine Diaries: Dispatches from Kiev.* New York: Random House, 2015.

Stephen Lendman, ed.   *Flashpoint in Ukraine: How the US Drive for Hegemony Risks World War III.* Atlanta, GA: Clarity Press, 2014.

Maria Lewytzkyj   *Putin's Putsches: Ukraine and the Near Abroad Crisis.* Miami, FL: Mango Media, 2014.

Paul Robert Magocsi   *A History of Ukraine: The Land and Its Peoples.* 2nd ed. Toronto: University of Toronto Press, 2010.

Paul Robert Magocsi   *Ukraine: An Illustrated History.* Toronto: University of Toronto Press, 2014.

Rajan Menon and Eugene B. Rumer   *Conflict in Ukraine: The Unwinding of the Post–Cold War Order.* Cambridge, MA: MIT Press, 2015.

Steven Pifer   *Averting Crisis in Ukraine.* New York: Council on Foreign Relations, 2009.

Serhii Plokhy   *Ukraine and Russia: Representations of the Past.* Toronto: University of Toronto Press, 2014.

Anna Reid   *Borderland: A Journey Through the History of Ukraine.* New York: Basic Books, 2015.

Gideon Rose   *Crisis in Ukraine.* Washington, DC: Council on Foreign Relations, 2014.

Richard Sakwa   *Frontline Ukraine: Crisis in the Borderlands.* London: I.B. Tauris, 2015.

Michael O. Slobodchikoff   *Building Hegemonic Order Russia's Way: Order, Stability, and Predictability in the Post-Soviet Space.* Lanham, MD: Lexington Books, 2014.

Marcel H. Van Herpen	*Putin's Wars: The Rise of Russia's New Imperialism.* Lanham, MD: Rowman & Littlefield, 2014.
Michael Wetzel	*The Ukrainian Crisis: A Call to Pray Big & Pray Bold.* Seattle, WA: CreateSpace, 2014.
Stephen White and Valentina Feklyunina	*Identities and Foreign Policies in Russia, Ukraine and Belarus: The Other Europes.* New York: Palgrave Macmillan, 2014.
Andrew Wilson	*Ukraine Crisis: What It Means for the West.* New Haven, CT: Yale University Press, 2014.

Index

CPSIA information can be obtained
at www.ICGtesting.com
Printed in the USA
FFOW05n1408151215